# 100+ TIPS FOR GETTING 100 FIVE STAR REVIEWS IN 100 DAYS

★★★★★

GROW YOUR PRACTICE AND GET MORE PATIENTS
BY TAKING ONE SIMPLE STEP EACH DAY

**DR. LEN TAU**

100+ Tips for Getting 100 Five Star Reviews in 100 Days
Grow Your Practice and Get More Patients By Taking One Simple Step Each Day

© 2022 Dr. Len Tau

All rights reserved. No portion of this book may be reproduced, stored in a retrieval system, or transmitted in any form or by any means—electronic, mechanical, photocopy, recording, scanning, or other—except for brief quotations in critical reviews or articles, without the prior written permission of the publisher.

ISBN Paperback: 979-8-9855021-2-1
ISBN eBook: 979-8-9855021-1-4

Cover Design by: 100covers.com
Interior Design by: formattedbooks.com

# CONTENTS

Foreword ................................................................................. v
Introduction ........................................................................... ix
How to Use this Book ........................................................ xiii

Tips 1 – 5: Getting The Most Value Out of This Book .................. 1

## HOW TO SET THE FOUNDATION FOR SUCCESS

Tips 6 – 11: Create an Environment That Earns You Reviews .......... 13
Tips 12 – 25: Focus on the Patient's Entire Experience With You .. 25
Tips 26 – 34: Ask for Reviews ................................................... 43
Tips 35 – 52: How to Make a Difference in Your Office Today ....... 57

## HOW TO UTILIZE ONLINE RESOURCES TO GET GREAT REVIEWS

Tips 53 – 58: General Tips ........................................................ 85
Tips 59 – 63: How to Use Email to Generate Reviews ................... 93
Tips 64 – 71: How to Use Google to Generate Reviews ................ 101
Tips 72 – 78: How to Use Facebook to Generate Reviews ............ 111
Tips 79 – 84: How to Use Yelp to Generate Reviews .................... 123
Tips 85 – 94: How to Use YouTube to Generate Reviews ............. 131
Tips 95 – 98: How to Use LinkedIn to Generate Reviews ............. 143
Tips 99 – 102: How to Use Your Website to Generate Reviews .... 149
Tips 103 – 109: How to Use Software to Generate Reviews ......... 155
Tips 110 – 125: How to Avoid Common Mistakes ...................... 165

Conclusion ........................................................................... 187
Acknowledgments ................................................................ 189
About the Author ................................................................. 191

# FOREWORD

When it comes to growing a dental practice—or any business for that matter—your reputation is king.

It doesn't matter how talented or organized you are, how clean your office is, or how sophisticated your marketing is, your long-term future depends on your reputation.

If your patients and others in your community have a positive impression of you and your business, your existing patients will stick around and refer you to friends and family.

Those referrals will then search for you on the internet before making an appointment.

When they do that, what will they see? Will they see mixed reviews? Will they see a steady flow of positive reviews? Will they see no reviews at all?

If they see mixed reviews or no reviews at all, they will be much more likely to ask another friend, family member, or colleague who they recommend. If they see a number of recent positive reviews they will be much more likely to reach out and schedule an appointment.

And what about when people look for dentists online? When people in your community search "dentist near me," does your practice come up on the map feature or on the first page of search results? Does your Google listing boast dozens of five-star reviews, letting the person know your practice is well liked and respected by its patients? Are you nowhere to be found? Or, do you come up with only a handful of reviews, mixed reviews, or only older reviews?

If your practice doesn't come up on the map or on the first page of search results showing a steady flow of five-star reviews, you're losing out on receiving dozens of new patients a month without having to spend a penny on expensive paid advertising.

Collecting a steady stream of five-star reviews doesn't need to be difficult, either. First, you need to make sure your practice deserves five-star reviews. Provide top-quality clinical care, operate a clean, organized practice, and treat your patients with care and respect. Second, you need to make collecting online reviews a simple, natural extension of your practice. You and your team members have enough to do taking care of patients and running your business. Collecting online reviews needs to be a simple enough process that it doesn't add even more work to your plates.

There's nobody more knowledgeable about collecting online reviews than Dr. Len Tau. As a dentist and practice owner for decades, Len has obtained the clinical and operational experience to know what it takes to earn a five-star reputation from patients while still operating a smooth, profitable practice. He also has extensive experience helping practices all around the country earn, collect, and use a steady flow of five-star reviews to grow their patient base.

In the pages that follow, you will find 100+ simple tips from Len and a select group of others hand-picked by Len to give you simple strategies that will help you and your team earn, collect, and promote your reviews. As you will see, each of the tips touches one small part of earning, collecting, and promoting reviews on a regular basis and can be implemented pretty easily by your or your team members with very little effort.

The best part about these tips is how simple they are to implement. In fact, some of the reviews might seem almost too simple but that's the point. In order to work, they need to be tips you can implement without adding even more work or complexity to your practice.

Whether you jump around or implement one tip after the other over a series of days doesn't matter. What does matter—for you, your team, and the future of your practice—is that you take action and start implementing the tips shared by Len in *100+ Tips for Getting 100 Five-Star Reviews in 100 Days* today.

Dr. Glenn Vo
NiftyThriftyDentists.com

# INTRODUCTION

Since 2013, it's been my mission to help dental professionals grow their practices by building their online reputation.

My name is Dr. Len Tau, but most folks call me the "Reviews Doctor." In 2020, I released my first book, *Raving Patients: The Definitive Guide to Using Reputation Marketing to Attract Hundreds of New Patients*.

Believe it or not, the "official gold standard" for your online reputation is a little more than 100 Google reviews. That doesn't seem like a crazy amount, right? Well, take it with a grain of salt. It sounds easy enough to collect that many reviews, but it's slightly more complicated than that, especially in the context of your competition. If your competitors have 500+ reviews, 100 won't look as impressive to potential patients.

You may have received reviews on other sites like Healthgrades, Yellow Pages, Facebook, or Yelp, each of which are valuable. However, you must collect and prioritize Google reviews specifically. Google reviews will help you gain further credibility, visibility, and ultimately, trust. While reviews on other sites are still helpful, focusing on gaining Google reviews will set the foundation and make it easier to get more reviews on the other platforms.

Reviews are important—there's no way around it. The more trust you gain from potential patients, the greater the chance they will choose you as their dental care provider. No prospective patient will choose you over the practice down the street unless there's a reason. Trusting a business based on their reviews is often cited by patients when they're choosing between practices and having a steady stream of reviews vouching for your practice is the best way to show how trustworthy you are.

You may think you have this area covered if you are using patient communication software like Lighthouse 360, Revenue Well, or Solution Reach. However, most, if not all, of the reviews will generally end up on sites like WebMD, Patient Connect 365, or Smile Reminder. None of those count in the race to the ultimate goal of reaching your "golden standard" of reviews.

It doesn't matter whether you're starting with zero, 25, 53, or 78 reviews on Google. You can only go up from wherever you currently are. These tips will help you keep adding to the tally. They're instructions for taking the steps necessary to unlock the keys to new patient acquisition.

As your review count increases, you will steadily be able to add other forms of marketing such as Pay-Per-Click Advertising (Google AdWords), sponsored Facebook posts, display advertising (retargeting), search engine optimization, and Facebook funnels. You will see a significant return on your investment, and your reputation will enhance the performance of those additional marketing avenues. The reviews are the fuel that allows the marketing to work so well. If you are contemplating marketing but don't have a lot of Google reviews, I would suggest holding off until you have a steady flow of reviews because you are wasting your money.

Today, consumers are more dependent on online reviews than ever before making a purchase.

Consider these stats from a 2020 BrightLocal[1] consumer survey:

- 79% of consumers trust online reviews as much as personal recommendations
- 87% of consumers read reviews for local businesses
- 86% of consumers only look at reviews from the past 3 months, 50% from the past two weeks
- 96% of consumers read local businesses' responses to reviews
- 88% of consumers would consider leaving reviews for businesses

In this quick reference guide, you will find 100+ tips to increase your online reviews by 100 or more in only 100 days. I'll start by teaching you the basic foundations of getting Google reviews, and then show you how you can use other platforms like Facebook and Yelp to boost your ratings.

## "Pro Tips" from Other Industry Experts and Practicing Dentists

In addition to tips from me, I reached out to other dental industry experts and practicing dentists and asked them to share their best tips for generating a steady flow of positive reviews.

You might recognize some of these contributors, whose tips are marked as "Pro Tips" throughout the book. Others, you might never have known about, as these practicing dentists keep busy serving their patients and building the culture, process, and relationships to generate five-star reviews.

---

[1] Rosie Murphy, "Local Consumer Review Survey 2020," BrightLocal, December 9, 2020, https://www.brightlocal.com/research/local-consumer-review-survey/.

Between my tips and the Pro Tips from industry experts and practicing dentists, you will find 100+ tips that can be implemented quickly at any practice. You most likely have thousands of happy patients that would be more than happy to talk about you online. Give them the ability to do that, make it easy for them, and help them become raving patients. These tips will not only be ways to generate reviews but things you can do to get *better* reviews.

But first, let's talk about how to use this book to get the most value out of it.

# HOW TO USE THIS BOOK

If you're reading this, you know reviews are important. But many dental professionals don't understand all the ways online reviews can help.

It doesn't matter how big or small your practice is, how many practices you own, or what your current reputation is (online or offline). None of these tips are unique to certain situations.

These tips do not require a lot of work to execute. You just need an open mind, an eager attitude, and a hard-working personality.

If you follow these tips, you will likely achieve a big uptick in leads. That's the good news. The bad news is that consistently attracting new patients to your dental practice is only one piece of the marketing puzzle. You also need to build a practice people love to visit and use your reviews strategically, a part of what I call reputation marketing. I talk all about reputation marketing in *Raving Patients: The Definitive Guide To Using Reputation Marketing To Attract Hundreds Of New Patients*, on my podcast, *Raving* Patients with Dr. Len Tau, and on my website, DrLenTau.com. If you want an even more in-depth examination of reviews and reputation marketing, you can find many options to work with me on my website.

This book is designed to help you collect the important building blocks for a successful marketing campaign: the reviews. We'll keep it short, sweet, and tactical. You won't be finding any dense bodies of long text to master. Just tactical action steps you can apply every day.

The dentists who get the best results from this book will be the ones who take action. The truth is, somebody in your area is working on building their reviews. And the more, the better, and the more consistent your reviews become, the more successful your practice can be. The only question is whether the person who is building their reviews in your area will be you or the practice owner down the street. It's as simple as that.

# TIPS 1 – 5

## GETTING THE MOST VALUE OUT OF THIS BOOK

As you are reading, feel free to take notes, write out your goals, or mark tips that you find especially helpful. Use the margins, separate sheets, you name it.

You can take it day-by-day and implement one tip per day. If you'd rather read and apply a handful at a time, that's fine, too. These tips are here to inform you and are designed to be simple to apply one at a time or in small groups; the rest is up to you. And while you might be able to breeze through the book in a day, I'd strongly encourage against it. This isn't a novel you read cover-to-cover and never think about again. It's a manual or handbook for you to look back on and take instructions from regularly. In the end, your results come from your actions. If you want more and better reviews, you need to take action.

As you'll see, you don't have to do it all yourself, either. Many tasks can be delegated to team members. And even if you only implement a few of the tips I recommend here, you can still see a huge positive impact on your business.

To see results, you need to take some steps, one step at a time. The first step toward building momentum is for everyone in your practice to get motivated, focused, and on the same page when it comes to collecting and using reviews. That's what we'll focus on next.

## TIP 1

# More Reviews, More Leads; More Leads, More New Patients

Did you know that 79% of consumers trust online reviews as much as personal recommendations? Building your reviews increases the likelihood a Google searcher will engage with your dental office upon finding it.

With the rise of the digital age, online reviews have become much more impactful and valued by potential patients. Having good reviews holds a lot of weight, as does having bad reviews.

However, it's better to have a few bad reviews than none at all. A few bad reviews make the good ones look even more genuine. Too many practice owners don't collect reviews because they're concerned about one or two bad ones.

Get started. Talk with your team about the impact of reviews on generating leads. Commit to building a positive environment that earns good reviews. That way, you can always get more good reviews to push down the bad ones. During your next team meeting or huddle let your team know you want to focus on collecting reviews from your happy patients.

# TIP 2

## Higher Reviews, Higher Rank

Do you want your practice's name to come up first in search results when a potential patient is looking for a dentist? For that to happen, you need to rank higher than your competitors in search results.

Google rewards businesses that have frequent and positive reviews. As confirmed by Google itself, reviews are a huge local SEO (search engine optimization) ranking factor.

That's why having a good rating and lots of positive reviews, especially on Google, is helpful. This will boost your practice to the top of the search results and increase the likelihood of patients choosing your office over another.

In other words, if you want to be higher on the results when someone googles "dentist near me," get more (and more consistent) reviews.

## TIP 3

## Pro Tip: Generating More Authentic Reviews

How can a dental office generate more authentic reviews from patients? Reviews are one of my favorite things. Why? Because they help me with my morale.

If my day isn't going well, and things aren't going my way, sometimes I'll read through my reviews. It's a good reminder of the appreciative patients I've previously helped, and a great mood booster.

Reviews are an opportunity to improve the morale of both the dentist and the team. They also allow patients to share stories of your awesomeness. The best way to do that is to authentically ask patients, "Would you help us help more patients just like you by sharing the story of your experience here? Believe it or not, we know not everyone loves the dentist as much as you."

So often, when you do that, your patients will oblige. People like to help people. That is the phrasing I use: "Would you help us help more patients just like you?" We ask them to tell patients how awesome dental care can be or how great it is to chew and smile with confidence.

We then make sure they know we truly appreciate it. Not everyone will do it, but it doesn't hurt to ask! People often feel very special when you ask them to share their story.

—Dr. Paul Goodman

A graduate of the University of Pennsylvania School of Dental Medicine, Dr. Paul Goodman has been practicing dentistry for over 10 years and works with his brother in two locations in Mercer County, NJ. Dr. Goodman has purchased three dental practices and shares his personal experience with retiring dentists in managing the expectations of their patients and team members during the transition process. He is the founder of Rising Dentists Study Club and Rittenhouse Consulting, LLC—both in Philadelphia. Learn more about Dr. Goodman at DentalNachos.com.

## TIP 4

## Pro Tip: Building Trust and Gaining Patients

Your online reputation is hugely influential, and, according to Becker's Hospital Review, 43% of these patients are reading your reviews after hours when your practice is closed.

If you combine those reviews with convenient real-time online scheduling, you can convert that trust into patient appointments, too.

A study by Healthgrades confirms that 83% of consumers already make travel and dinner reservations online, and 80% of them would prefer to book healthcare appointments online; only 15% of all healthcare appointments today are made online via real-time scheduling.

Dentists today have a tremendous opportunity to differentiate themselves from the competition, leverage their stellar online reputation, and gain even more five-star reviews by offering convenient access patients want and use.

Collecting and highlighting your reviews and adding 24/7 scheduling on your site might mean the difference between a patient scheduling with you or with the dentist down the block who uses that combination on their site.

—Gina Dorfman

Gina Dorfman DDS is a practicing dentist and the founder of Dentistry for Kids and Adults, a busy family practice just north of Los Angeles, California. She is also a cofounder and the CEO of the paperless dental software company, Yapi. Contact her at drgina@yapicentral.com

## TIP 5

## Lots of Reviews, Lower Costs, More Social Proof

One of the best things about online reviews is they are free.

Patients don't have to pay anything to leave a review, and you don't have to pay a penny to collect or respond to Google reviews.

Positive endorsements for your business on your Business Profile serve as free Google advertising for your business on the world's most trusted platform.

Contrast that with other ways to promote your practice, such as through paid advertisements: if a prospect is seeing your advertisement, they're usually aware you're a biased source of information—you're selling to them, after all.

Reviews from patients come across as less biased and much more authentic. They hold a lot more weight than what you say about your practice through an advertisement.

They act as what's called "social proof" in the marketplace: proof that other people find you valuable. Other examples of social proof are when you receive an award, are featured on the news, or earn an accolade in your community.

Social proof is one of the most effective factors in any marketing effort.

That's why utilizing Google reviews is so helpful. It's using free word-of-mouth advertising digitally.

# HOW TO SET THE FOUNDATION FOR SUCCESS

★★★★★

# TIPS 6 – 11

## CREATE AN ENVIRONMENT THAT EARNS YOU REVIEWS

## TIP 6

## Create a Reputation Culture in Your Office

The first and most important step to earning positive reviews is creating a reputation culture for your practice. To get more reviews, the entire office must be onboard—from the front desk to the hygienist to even the dentist. If your team isn't on the same page, you won't see results. The entire team needs to be committed to this new way of thinking.

Your patients are tuned into how you make them feel throughout every step of their visit. That means you are performing at the top of your game for every single patient. Treat each patient as though you're the owner of a restaurant and they're high-profile food critics in disguise. You can't be providing lackluster results to anybody—especially if you're counting on their review.

When you cross over that threshold at the front door, all the problems in your life must go away. You need to put on a happy face, represent the practice, and put your best foot forward. From the time you answer the phone to the time a patient leaves the practice, be on your A-game.

Your whole dental team needs to be making a conscious effort to impress all your patients. If they do, your patients will get a feel for your practice as soon as they walk in. Make sure you are creating the environment and culture that will have your patients leaving impressed.

## TIP 7

# Give Them Something to Talk About

"Give them something to talk about" is not just from a Bonnie Raitt song. If you do something cool, it can inspire people to talk about your business.

Give your patients an extraordinary experience when they come to your practice. If you do, they'll want to scream from the rooftops about all the amazing aspects of your office. On the other hand, if you give your patients just an ordinary experience, they'll leave your practice feeling indifferent. They won't have many positive things to say about your practice.

What are you doing to make the patient's experience extraordinary?

It doesn't take much to show your patients you care. Some small ideas you can implement are checking in personally with your patients after their procedures. You can give them a phone call, send a "get well" card, or deliver flowers to their house.

Another idea is spicing up the environment of your office by investing in some mood enhancers. You can upgrade your office by adding a mini fridge stocked with drinks and snacks in the waiting room. You can invest in massage chairs for your patients. Even just buying an essential oil diffuser to set a positive mood can go a long way.

Patients will take note of the little things. If you want to stand out amongst all other dentists in your area, dedicate some time to implementing factors in your office that will set you apart from the rest.

## TIP 8

## Pro Tip: Positive Reviews Begin with a Positive Patient Experience–From First Contact

Impressions are made quickly, and your practice will either start the new patient relationship on the right foot or with a deficit to overcome. The secret to ensuring the first impression will be a good one? Honestly evaluating what it's like to be a new patient in your practice.

Start online. Is your website user-friendly, with essential information front and center? Is it easy to request or schedule an appointment without speaking to someone (today's patients hate talking on the phone!)?

When someone calls, will the friendliest person they've ever talked to pick up the phone? Are you answering phones during the times most convenient for your patients—during their lunch hour, for example? Are your new patient forms easy and fast to complete on all devices? Are your no-compromise appointment and payment policies clearly and politely communicated with no future surprises?

Sit in your waiting area. Is it clean, comfortable, attractive, and welcoming? Is your front office team friendly, attentive, and professional? Are you creating the best, patient-focused experience possible?

Happy patients are much more willing to forgive the rare negative if you've spent time focusing on a phenomenal first impression and committing to keeping that positive experience consistent for every interaction moving forward.

—Scott Childress, co-founder, CEO,
Magnify Dental Marketing

For over a decade, Scott has directed the development of websites, social media accounts, local search listings, and review-building campaigns for over 1,000 dentists across forty-seven states and six countries. Today, Scott directs a growing team of marketing experts through Magnify, a dental marketing company he co-founded in early 2020.

## TIP 9

## Pro Tip: Send Handwritten Letters

Send a handwritten card to each new patient after their first visit. Make it personal by including something you and your patient spoke about during their visit.

For example, if they shared a story about something positive that happened in their personal life, congratulate them again. If they talked about an upcoming family trip, wish them safe travels.

At the end of the letter, ask for a review to help you find more great patients like them!

Patients love a personalized handwritten card.

—Dawn Patrick

With over 30 years of experience in the dental field, Dawn Patrick offers virtual services to dental practices. Whether you are a new dental practice, established practice, or a dental consultant, Dawn can provide virtual support for your business and marketing needs.

# TIP 10

## Pro Tip: Create "Touchpoints"

In my dental practice, Crossroads Dental Arts, we try to hit as many touchpoints as we can to get our patients to "rave" about the practice and give us great reviews. Every interaction between a patient and your practice is considered a "touchpoint," such as how the patient is greeted when they arrive, the phone call prior to the new patient appointment, having insurance verified, performing a thorough exam and giving a detailed treatment plan, running on time, providing amenities to the patient, and giving a new patient gift.

By focusing on making every touchpoint a positive experience, my practice has been able to amass 2,300 reviews.

When you have systems or even a focus in place to "touch" patients in positive ways at every interaction with your practice, you will never have to worry about not having enough great reviews. People will be happy to share their fantastic experience on the web.

Here is a sample of a recent review that a new patient left for us on Google that mentions the experiences she had. We cannot ask for a better review than this!

"Highly recommended! Came in for a cleaning and check on some soreness with a root canal from a different dentist. From the moment I walked in, I was greeted with the kindest energy from Donelle (who called ahead of time to make sure I had everything I needed) at the front desk and seen right on time. Very knowledgeable about my provider plan and verified everything beforehand so there were no unexpected costs. The Drs were fantastic as well, did a thorough job with X-rays/gum testing/ cleaning and were very transparent with their plan to address the soreness with my crown, even going as far as providing me a printout of the plan and breakdown of cost by my provider and what would be owed on my copay. Very straight forward, and very prompt, taking just about an hour. The office was modern and spotless clean, offered free water/juice (protip, OJ before cleaning not after LOL), and sent me on my way with a lovely care package. I'll be referring my partner here in the future and I would recommend Crossroads to anyone out there!"

—Dr. Joanne Block Rief, Crossroad Dental Arts

For 18 years, Dr. Rief practiced with her father and mother (who was the office manager). In 2004, she purchased a small dental practice, which she has since grown and evolved into a state-of-the-art facility that allows her and her team members to give her patients the best possible dental care.

## TIP 11

## Provide Review-Worthy Service

A big part of the last few tips revolves around the same principle: provide review-worthy service.

This may seem obvious, but it is one thing that a lot of practices miss when trying to grow their reviews. They focus too much on the process and not enough on the foundation.

You can use all the tricks in the book (and in this book) to bring in reviews, but they won't help you if you don't provide a stellar service or product worthy of those reviews. If no one is satisfied with your office, no one will want to leave you a positive review.

Make sure your customer service is up to snuff and that your products are satisfactory. Consistently going above and beyond what patients expect and truly impressing them with your service will motivate them to leave glowing reviews on Google. It will get them to come back to you in the future and build the kind of loyalty every local business needs to thrive. You'll begin bringing in reviews organically and the rest of these tips will help you encourage more.

# TIPS 12 – 25

## FOCUS ON THE PATIENT'S ENTIRE EXPERIENCE WITH YOU

## TIP 12

## Ask Your Patients to Use Google Maps to Get Directions to Your Office

If your patients use Google Maps to get directions to your office, Google will know that they have been in your office. After your patient has left, they will send the patient a review request unless this feature has been turned off in your Google Business Profile account.

This makes it much easier to collect reviews without having to put in much effort. It also gives you more opportunities, especially because it's Google asking, not you and your staff directly.

For example, this tip could be implemented by training your front desk team members to make it a part of patient conversations. Let's say your front desk team member is calling a patient to remind them about treatment. They might say, "If you're unsure of the fastest way to get here with real-time traffic taken into account, we've found it's easier to use Google Maps. But if you'd just prefer our address and our office number, I can provide that." This doesn't seem pushy or salesy at all, and it's getting the point across to the patient: "Why not use Google Maps?"

Get creative. If your front desk team member is following up with a patient rather than reminding them of an appointment, they'd just need to frame the conversation a little differently. Instead, they might ask whether the patient got to the practice okay. Regardless of whether the ride over was like navigating a maze or it was a few simple turns, the front desk team member can still recommend using Google Maps for next time.

# TIP 13

## Educate Your Patients on How to Leave a Review

More often than you'd expect, your patients want to leave you a review but don't know where to start. Sometimes, you need to hold their hand and show them how.

Offer to have your patient take out their phone and you can show them how to do it in person if they express having some difficulty. For many people, the barrier between them leaving a review or not is knowing how to do so.

By showing them directly, not only does it show your dedication and attention to care, but you will be much more likely to get a review from that person.

FYI: Taking the phone from them and tapping on the stars is not showing them It's doing it for them. Don't do that. Why am I writing this? I have seen this done before.

## TIP 14

### Pro Tip: Get Personal

Follow up with patients you saw that day.

I often call patients in the evening and follow up with them, especially those who had more extensive work. Give them a call to check in, see how they're doing.

So many patients are shocked when they realize the dentist is calling them personally. When they express their thanks and tell you how impressed they are you are calling them, that's the absolute best time to ask for a review.

It's been my #1 method for getting reviews.

—Dr. Eric Moryoussef

A graduate of the University of Toronto Faculty of Dentistry, Dr. Eric Moryoussef is honored to serve the Fort Erie and greater Niagara communities at Riverside Dental Centre. Dr. Eric has been recognized for his excellence in dentistry by the Edward G. Dore Award and the Oral Anatomy Scholarship, and has been recognized for his community contributions with the Gordon Cressy Leadership Award.

## TIP 15

## Emphasize to Your Patients How Quick and Easy It Is

By now, you know how easy it is to leave a Google review, but your patients may not. Plus, review writer's block is a thing.

An exuberant or long-time patient may have a hard time distilling everything they love about your office into one review. Some may have a hard time articulating what's on their mind. When you're encouraging a review, it might be helpful to:

- ➢ Tell them they can leave a star rating without writing anything (if applicable).
- ➢ Remind them that if they do write, the review needs only be one or two sentences.
- ➢ Use terminology like "leave a review" or "drop a quick review" instead of "write a review," as it might feel less cumbersome. For those that know me, I recommend asking for feedback about the patient's experience.

## TIP 16

## Identify Potential Reviewers

An effective way to identify potential reviewers is to ask your patients how they found you. If they found you on a review site, there is a strong possibility that they will be more than happy to write a review for you as well.

Whenever a patient mentions they chose my office because of my reviews, I always mention to them that they will be receiving a request for one. They're normally more than happy to oblige.

Framing conversations with current patients around how they found you can help you determine where to focus your efforts. If they found you through your social media, for example, you can spend some time planning out engaging content to attract new patients. If they found you through a Google search for a dentist, you know you are headed in the right direction and should continue to get more reviews.

# TIP 17

## Pro Tip: Two Ears, One Mouth

Listen for a compliment.

Keep your ears open and wait for any praise about your practice.

Use the appreciation as a way to open the conversation about the patient writing a review about that specific compliment.

The music in the office, how it smells; it doesn't matter.

Train your team to pounce when a patient compliments something about the office.

—Dr. Joshua Austin, Columnist at Dental Economics Magazine and Dentist at Joshua Austin DDS

Joshua Austin, DDS, MAGD, FACD, is a graduate of San Antonio's Health Careers High School, the University of Texas San Antonio, and the University of Texas Health Science Center San Antonio Dental School, one of the top-ranked dental schools in the nation since 1993. Dr. Austin excelled in dental school and was voted president of his graduating class. He capped off a successful senior year by being awarded the Texas Dental Association Outstanding Senior Dental Student award.

# TIP 18

## Pro Tip: Delegate to Appreciate

After we have spent time, energy, and money to get reviews, it is important we acknowledge those reviews. Replying to the reviews is a great starting point, but we can go one step further. Here's a simple and effective strategy for leveraging reviews.

Assign a team member to check all your reviews on a weekly basis. Have the team member add all the positive reviews by current patients in their patient charts and make a note to acknowledge the review at their next appointment. Inform all team members who will be speaking with the patient to say thank you for the review.

This will let your patients know that you not only read the review but shared it with the entire team. They will be more willing to share more reviews about your practice and refer new patients. Your current patients are one of your top referrals for new patients, so why not make sure they feel appreciated?

—Minal Sampat

Minal Sampat, RDH, BA, has spent over a decade helping practices reach their goals through effective, strategic, easy-to-implement marketing strategies. Whether it's getting more patients in the door, strengthening your team, or growing your business, Minal can help. Learn more at MinalSampat.com.

# TIP 19

## Pro Tip: Text and Call Patients at Night

If the patient is younger, I text.

If they are older, I call.

I ask how they're doing and make sure they're feeling well.

Then, for my text, I send a Google review link and ask them for a favor to leave a review.

If they're older, I ask them over the phone.

The best time to text or call patients is at night. They'll be home and more likely to leave you a review if you contact them at night.

—Dr. Meenal Patel, Preston Dental Loft

Highly regarded as a cosmetic clinician, Dr. Meenal Patel, DMD, FAGD, FICOI, has advanced training in cosmetic dentistry, orthodontics, endodontics, prosthodontics, and dental implantology with additional certifications in Invisalign and Six Month Smiles treatment. She has been awarded the prestigious Fellowship in the Academy of General Dentistry as well as Fellowship in the International Congress of Oral Implantologists.

## TIP 20

## Ask for Feedback Using a Review Service

Ask every patient who leaves about their experience.

Say, "Thanks for coming in today. We hope you had a great experience!" If they respond positively, ask them to leave a review.

From there, using a review service like BirdEye will make it even easier and put the process on autopilot.

When they reply positively, respond, "Just so you know, you may be receiving a text message asking for feedback about your experience, we look forward to reading what you have to say."

If they respond negatively, it might be better to not ask for their feedback. It likely wouldn't be positive. You would be better off asking for private feedback in the moment.

# TIP 21

## Ask for Feedback from Facebook Users

To collect reviews on Facebook, be specific.

At the end of an appointment, ask each patient for feedback. Keep it simple. Just say, "Thanks for coming in today. How was your experience?"

If positive, respond, "Great. Do you have a Facebook account? We would appreciate you taking the time to share your feedback by writing a review for us on Facebook. If you have any questions for us, please let us know."

By being specific, it's more likely they'll actually hop on the app and leave a review. They might even do it then and there. Take it a step further by offering to text them the link to your Facebook page so they can go directly to Facebook the next time they use their phone.

## TIP 22

### Ask for Feedback from Android Phone Users

Android phone users are some of the most valuable reviewers.

Why? Because, although it's technically possible to use an Android phone without a Google account, virtually all Android users have Google accounts linked to their phones.

Thus, be on the lookout for Samsung and other Android phones. As those patients leave your practice, ask them to leave a review on Google.

Keep it simple by saying, "Thanks for coming in today. How was your experience?" If positive, respond, "Great, would you be willing to leave a Google review for us? We would appreciate it and, with Android phones, it is really easy for you to be able to write us a Google review to share your experience."

If they say yes, you can thank them and offer to send them a text reminder with a link to your Google Business Profile page (formerly called your Google My Business page until Google renamed it in late 2021).

(You can check out Tips 64-71 for specific tips and tricks for utilizing Google.)

# TIP 23

## Ask in Response to Praise

As Dr. Joshua Austin mentioned in his Pro Tip, the easiest scenario in which you can ask for a review involves a patient who approaches you with unsolicited praise.

This happens often in many practices, so I want to share my approach here, too.

In this case, express your appreciation for their taking the time to provide the feedback, and then make the suggestion to leave a review.

You might say something like: "That is so great to hear. We try our best to [do what you're being praised for]. Thank you so much for taking the time to provide your feedback."

Your patient might respond with something like, "For sure, thank you for providing such great service!"

You can follow with, "You know, those kinds of comments help prospective patients feel more confident in choosing us. If you don't mind writing what you just said in a quick review on [platform of your choice], that would be awesome."

## TIP 24

## Create Opportunities by Striking Up a Conversation

If a patient doesn't offer praise on their own, ask them about their experience at their checkout process using phrases such as:

- ➢ "How was your cleaning or filling today?"
- ➢ "How was your first visit to the office today?"
- ➢ "Do you love the results of the whitening?"

It's important to note that you shouldn't ask for a review upon their first positive remark about your office. This will render your conversation ingenuine and you will come off as not caring about their experience but rather just about getting the review. But you can ask them for additional specifics.

Get a read on the patient. If their response is short and indicative, suggesting they don't feel like talking, don't force it. If they respond positively and offer more information or feedback, continue the conversation. As it comes to a close, you can then feel comfortable asking for the review.

"Well, hey, thanks for the feedback. We love sharing that kind of stuff with potential patients so they can feel more comfortable with choosing us. If you're comfortable with it, it'd be awesome if you could share what you said to me in an online review."

# TIP 25

## Pro Tip: Three Steps to Getting Excellent Reviews

Here are 3 steps to get excellent reviews:

1. **Make sure your patients have a great experience from their appointment or treatment.**

It's all about the experience. If your patients like and trust you and your team, then most likely they will go the extra mile to endorse your business through their reviews.

2. **You or your team member should ask your satisfied patients to share his/her feedback about their positive experience.**

If you want to get great reviews for your business, especially reviews that have stories and experiences, then you must ask. If not, you may get some reviews but most of these reviews won't have much writing in them that mention their experience or your business.

3. **You should simplify the process for your patients to write their reviews.**

These are simple steps but very effective in generating great reviews for your business. Remember, your business' online reviews are your business' online reputation. Having more and better reviews than your competitors is the best way to dominate your online market and attract more patients to your practice.

—Dr. Nathan Ho

Dr. Nathan Ho is a dentist, a serial entrepreneur, and marketing strategist. Currently, he is a practicing dentist; the co-founder and CEO of EnvisionStars, a business builder software company; the founder and CEO of DentalMedPPE.com, a dental supply company; and the host of the Dental WinWin Summit, a business and clinical continuing education program for dentists.

# TIPS 26 – 34

## ASK FOR REVIEWS

# TIP 26

## Start to Just ASK

Asking patients for a review has the lowest cost to the practice. That said, it's also very inefficient.

Even if your patients agree to leave a review, many of them will not follow through.

That means you have to ask more patients than you might want to.

You need to ask a lot of patients.

That means looking for reasons to ask. Like mentioned above, looking for praise or other opportunities to ask can help.

But you need to create your own opportunities as well.

Ask patients during every interaction with your practice, and not just after treatment.

If a patient calls to handle an administrative issue and expresses gratitude for helping resolve the issue, ask.

If a patient refers a new patient to you, call them to thank them and ask.

Look for all the opportunities to ask for feedback in the form of a review.

# TIP 27

## Have the Dentist Ask

A lot of the time, your dental team will begin feeling uncomfortable asking every single patient for a review or feedback. They start feeling too pushy when they're saying it after every visit.

It makes sense that they don't want to seem too forward or come off as aggressive—we're in healthcare, not sales. But we can't serve patients if they can't find us. And having a steady flow of reviews coming in is your ticket to getting a steady flow of patients coming in.

One solution is having the doctor ask for reviews themselves. There's something about the dentist doing it that seems to generate better results. Maybe it's that they seem busier. Maybe it feels like an order coming directly from the top.

I present treatment and financials in my office and have a lot of success. When I ask patients to write a review, they seem to do it more often. It only takes a couple of seconds after the appointment and it can have amazing results. Try it out and see what happens. You may be in for quite a surprise.

## TIP 28

### Be Consistent With Asking

Let's say a regular patient is coming in for a six-month hygiene visit.

They're going to interact with the hygienist, the dentist who is examining the patient, and the receptionist who is checking the patient out of the office as well as welcoming them to the practice. If the patient needs some restorative work, they may also see the assistants during the visit.

There are lots of opportunities for your dental staff and you to ask about the patient's experience and go out of your way to provide the best care.

Is asking for feedback part of your routine process with patients? If not, consider adding it to your standard process to ensure you and your staff consistently ask for feedback.

Patients will normally talk about their experiences with you before they leave the office. And getting both positive feedback and constructive criticism in real time makes consistent improvement easier for you and your team.

Get patients used to you and your team asking for feedback. That way, it becomes a natural part of each visit.

Finally, make sure you note which patients have recently left a review as well because this is a perfect opportunity to ask them to write a review.

# TIP 29

## Ask a Patient to Write a Review on an Aftercare Call

Firstly, make sure that you are calling to check in on your patients after procedures. Not only is this a great way to build a stronger relationship with patients and show you care, but you can create an opportunity to talk about their experience in your practice and lead to a review.

Any time you anesthetize a patient, do an aftercare call to see how they are feeling. If they respond favorably, you can let them know you would appreciate them writing a review for you on Google or even offer to send them a text or email to make it easy.

The more you're able to reach out, connect with your patients, and show you care, the more opportunities you'll have to get more reviews.

If you are using a software program you can also mention to the patient at this time that they will be getting a text asking them to write a review or leave feedback whichever you prefer.

## TIP 30

### Make it Convenient

The tricks in this book are centered around getting your patients to write you a Google review. Sometimes a patient might not have a Google account, or they may not be technologically savvy enough to navigate Google. In that case, it's too "out of their way" to leave a review.

It makes sense. Just think about how inconvenient it is to leave a Google review if you don't even have an account. You need to go through a step-by-step process that can strip minutes off your day. Most folks have the time, but it's just not worth it to them—they have more pressing matters to attend.

Not all reviews are created equal, as we've discussed, and Google reviews are the cream of the crop. But beggars can't be choosers, so to speak. If you ask for a review only to discover your patient doesn't know the slightest thing about Google, ask them if they're familiar with any other platforms. That's much better than asking them to create an account.

Don't make it more complicated than it needs to be. That'll frustrate the patient if anything, and it's unlikely anybody is willing to let a simple review for a dental practice inconvenience them. The moment things seem complicated, they'll probably think it isn't worth the effort.

# TIP 31

## Remind Patients How Helpful Reviews Can Be

Sometimes patients don't understand how helpful it is for practices when they leave a review. Once they do, they are more likely to leave you a review.

Thus, one way to get patients to be more likely to leave a review is to make that connection for them.

Simple and direct communication is best. You or your team members could even be as blunt as saying, "Let me ask you a direct question. Do you consider yourself a helpful person?"

Most people will say yes. Then you can continue with: "It's incredibly helpful to me personally when patients I see leave positive reviews online. It lets other people know how hard we work to give you the best experience possible. Would you be willing to help me out by leaving a review on Google when you get home today?"

You could also end the request by saying, "We would love to have you go online and write a review on Google for us. Can we count on you to do this when you get home today?"

Another option: "Thanks for coming in today. Just so you know, you may be receiving an email or text today that will ask you to provide some feedback about your experiences in our office today. It helps us out personally and as a practice when patients share their positive experiences in the form of a Google review. We would appreciate you taking the time to do this when you get home today."

Patients want to be helpful. Many consider themselves helpful people. They just don't know how helpful it is to take two minutes to write an online review.

# TIP 32

## Timing, Timing, Timing

Be smart when you ask for your review.

Don't rush it. You want to time the review perfectly to when the patient is in the best mood and most willing to write a review.

Knowing when to ask for a review plays a crucial part in getting more reviews and more positive reviews.

Don't ask for a review before you've built enough rapport with the patient. You can ask for feedback but don't ask for a review until you've built some rapport.

Treat them with care and respect through multiple touchpoints.

Then look for opportunities to ask when they are pleased with their interaction with your practice.

## TIP 33

### Create a Review Instruction Video

Even with asking or sending your patients a text message, some patients will be more likely to write a review if they see what the process looks like.

In this case, creating a quick video on how to leave a Google Review for your business may be just what you need.

Simply recording your phone or computer screen and explaining what they need to do will now make it even easier for your patient.

If you want to see what this could look like, visit the resources page at resources.drlentau.com where you will find one I recorded. Feel free to use mine or make your own.

# TIP 34

## Pro Tip: Create a Fun Place to Work

We at Progressive Dental spend quite a bit of time and resources on our culture and employee's happiness factors. When your team members are happy, your patients will benefit. Thus, focus on creating a fun place to work first, and you'll have a much easier time getting patients to leave positive reviews.

In short, we want our office to be a fun place to work and play. The sound of laughter is heard often, and I can't tell you how many times we've seen that mentioned in a review. You can't take yourself too seriously. Patients that are nervous will see right through it and will not be able to relate to you.

We also encourage our team to connect on a one-on-one basis with patients. The last four reviews we've gotten in the last three days all mentioned someone on our team who made them feel at ease, by being themselves and listening intently and responding like a normal, compassionate person would and not someone who is paid to be there. We talk about it at morning meetings and reinforce it daily.

I strive to show gratitude toward my team daily, and vocally in front of patients. A simple "thank you for taking care of this" goes miles. Showing respect for your team will translate into respect for your patients.

—Sonny Spera

Dr. Spera purchased his practice in 1991 and has grown it into five fee-for-services offices across New York and Northeast Pennsylvania with seven doctors, and more than 70 staff members. Dr. Spera is loving life with his wife of 35 years, Angela, and their three children, Marcus, Erica, and Carla.

# TIPS 35 – 52

## HOW TO MAKE A DIFFERENCE IN YOUR OFFICE TODAY

## TIP 35

### Pro Tip: Quality Over Quantity

If you're new to online marketing, search engine optimization, or SEO, is the process of getting websites ranked higher on search engines. This improves both the quality and quantity of website traffic. SEO is typically an unpaid marketing strategy, as compared to Search Engine Marketing, or SEM, in which you pay to have your website featured as an advertisement for certain search queries.

In the world of SEO, there's a concept known as "long-tail search."

Long-tail searches are search terms or phrases that are typically longer and more descriptive search queries. While long-tail searches will have lower levels of search volume, statistically they are much higher converting searchers—those much more likely to engage with your business. These are people who are looking for something very specific, and when they find what they are looking for, they take action.

So why should this matter to you?

It should matter greatly.

When patients leave you reviews, those reviews have potential valuable keywords and phrases that Google can extract.

When it comes to asking patients for reviews, don't just send emails and text messages to your patients "asking for feedback" or to "please leave a review." This would drive the blandest response, if any at all. Instead, try asking for the review in a different way. For example:

"Hi (Name) - We would like to know if anyone at our practice today delivered an amazing experience to you? Please leave them a review!"

"Hi (Name) - Did we exceed your expectations today? If so, please tell us more!"

"Hi (Name) - What was the best part of your visit today? It's important for us to know your experience was nothing short of amazing."

"Hi (Name) - We must be doing something right! Let us know what keeps you coming back to see Dr. Jones."

By asking for reviews more pointedly you will undoubtedly get more insightful, keyword-rich, user-generated content. In time, this will undoubtedly help drive more local visibility, brand awareness, and other new patients through your door.

It's not quantity you're after, it's quality.

—Evan Lazarus

Evan Lazarus did not become a marketer the way most do. He went to Wall Street, started trading stocks and options, built a hedge fund, grew it to over $200M, and then one day, decided to walk away from it all. In 2017, Evan launched Simple Impact Media as a boutique marketing and consulting firm that specializes in local search, web design, and digital advertising. He was named one of twenty-five people in the Philadelphia area shaping hyperlocal marketing.

## TIP 36

## Get Reviews From Vendors and Other Industry Partners

Vendors and partners may not be patients, but they can attest to what it's like to work with you regularly. Although it isn't a review from a patient, a partner or vendor review can give potential patients a feel for the culture of your practice.

Building strong relationships with vendors and partners is beneficial for your practice, too. When you establish meaningful connections with vendors and partners, you can continue to support and promote each other throughout your careers.

You might consider making the first move and leaving a review for their businesses first. If you put good out into the world, it will come back to you.

# TIP 37

## Use Incentives to Get Reviews

Sometimes, your team can't consistently ask for reviews. Delegating it to your team simply isn't a sustainable business model. They have too many things to do during the daily operations of running a dental practice.

You can't incentivize the patient to give reviews in any way, shape, or form, either. Bribing them to leave a review on Google violates the terms of service and risks having your reviews taken down.

But you *can* incentivize your staff.

For example, you could incentivize your team with a spa day if they get 25 Google reviews in a month. Those 25 reviews will have a profound effect online, meaning the spa day expenses will get paid back tenfold. Even if they don't reach that 25, every review is helpful and every effort toward getting those reviews counts.

Your entire team may not be on board, but you may be able to get a single employee who wants to make a little extra money. Offer this team member a monetary incentive for each review received. This may be all you need to up your review game.

# TIP 38

## Pro Tip: Be Organic

Truly the best way to get reviews is organically.

Do your very best in the customer service area, in the painless dentistry area, and the quality care area and the reviews will happen realistically. Trying to generate reviews is often transparent. I used to dread the occasional bad review, but these outliers only serve to make our profile look realistic.

When all you have is five-star reviews, your profile loses credibility. Even with a few negative reviews, we still have an overall five-star rating, so I speak with a little experience.

—Dr. Josh Bernstein, DDS, All New Smiles

Dr. Bernstein served as a Senior Clinical Instructor on the faculty at LVI. As a Clinical Instructor, he taught dentists from around the globe about the latest techniques in cosmetic dentistry, full mouth reconstruction, and other advanced dental treatment. He is the author of *The Book on Painless Dentistry* and the Founder and President of The Dental Comfort Academy. Learn more about Dr. Bernstein at AllNewSmiles.com.

## TIP 39

## Connect With a Local Celebrity or Influencer

Influencers have a huge impact on people nowadays. Social media in general is one of the best ways to promote your practice.

Finding local bloggers is a great way to generate more reviews for your business. While all user reviews are valuable, a favorable review from an influencer in your area or industry carries a significant value for potential patients.

First, begin looking for bloggers with a large following on social media in your area. Then, reach out to them and offer them something of value, such as a complimentary teeth whitening session, in return for promoting your practice on their platform. This will have a huge weight online and can bring in more patients.

## TIP 40

### Run a Contest

This is somewhat in the gray area category. You are not allowed to *incentivize* someone to give you a review, but you can enter someone who leaves a review into a contest to win something.

This could be anything from a gift card to an Apple watch; find something of value and offer it to those patients who write a review for you. Then, announce the winner on your social media channels.

This will help you build stronger online relationships as well as in-person with your patients and certainly engage more people on your social media. When your followers on social media see that someone who left you a review won an Apple watch, they will likely want to leave you a review, too.

# TIP 41

## Pro Tip: Give a Review, Get a Review

I have used the "give a review, get a review" tactic in my offices to much success.

We would take photos of patients who would allow it (including pediatric patients).

My office would write a sincere and personalized blurb about the patient, their case, the great outcome, and how much we love serving them. We would often include a quote from the patient.

The "patient review" would be posted wherever the patient would allow it, from Facebook to beyond.

We also even helped patients enter personal competitions, from beauty to dental-specific. The idea is to give first before we ask.

When we do, the patient often "returns the favor" and writes a five-star review of the practice.

The reviews are more genuine than if you "pay to play," as the patients express themselves from their emotional sides more than anything else. It's all about a positive experience and attitude and the only way to get that is to earn it.

—Jeremy Krell, DMD, MBA

Dr. Jeremy Krell is a general dentist, as well as an experienced investor with a business background. He has raised rounds and generated returns for investors at ten companies, sold three, and acquired two more as a key operator. Jeremy oversaw strategic provider innovation and development at Oscar Health, a health insurance company that had an IPO in 2021. He also led provider and clinical growth initiatives at quip, a subscription oral health company, and has since built the Barchester Bay Group, a portfolio consisting of over thirty separate ventures. Jeremy is an angel investor and sits on the boards of several healthcare and dental startups. He has over fifteen years of a proven track record with start-ups, multi-million dollar fundraises, and acquisitions. You can learn more about Dr. Krell at ReverePartnersSVC.com.

## TIP 42

## Spread the Words With Friends and Family

If (and only if) you have treated your friends and family as patients, you should ask them to leave a review.

If you're looking for a jump start, ask your family and friends who are patients of yours to post reviews for your practice.

Note that it toes the line of what is acceptable and what is not for local review sites, but as long as the reviews are sincere and come across that way, it shouldn't be a problem.

Then, ask your family and friends to spread the word to anyone they know who has used or interacted with your practice to leave a review as well.

Because it's easier to ask friends and family, some practice owners can get a jump start on their reviews this way. With any luck, several of them will post reviews and you can start building momentum right away.

## TIP 43

## Show Your Reviews on a TV in the Reception Area

While your patients are waiting in the reception area, use a TV to promote your online reviews.

You can showcase some of the best reviews you have received. You can also show where they left the review, and a step-by-step guide to how the patients waiting can write one, too.

While your patients and your patient's family or friends are waiting, they usually have a good amount of spare time.

This is the perfect time to ask for a review; even if they haven't gone in to see you yet, they've likely been there before and can base a review off the service they have already received.

Here's an example of a business promoting their Yelp! review on a TV.

COVID-19 may have eliminated your reception area but you may still have a TV so you can still promote those great reviews you are getting.

AS SEEN ON yelp
Stopped here after driving past it 900 times, best decision ever.
Everything was incredible, the wait was long so we sat at the bar
and once we met Daly and she made a Knob Creek old fashioned to
PERFECTION we stayed.
The food was exponentially better than anticipated and the service
was outstanding. I almost didn't want to post this because more people
would come here LOL! The volcano shrimp beats any bang bang shrimp
I've ever had. Burrata was to die for and the onion soup-forget about it.
So in love with this place!
Meagan W.
DISABLED
ASSISTANCE
UPON REQUEST
MAXIMUM
OCCUPANCY 260

## TIP 44

## Get Testimonials From Patients Who Were at First Skeptical of Buying

Rather than asking for testimonials from your patients who immediately fell in love with you and your practice, try to look for those that were at first skeptical about your practice or the procedure they were having.

If a patient shares that they were skeptical but pleased, prospective patients with similar skepticism will be more willing to give your practice a chance.

# TIP 45

## Don't Forget to Follow Up After Asking

To dental professionals, forgoing treatment is a form of blasphemy. We can't neglect our teeth! However, our patients live busy lives. They aren't as aware of the role that good oral health can play in our overall well-being, and sometimes they don't prioritize it. For that reason, most practice owners have learned to follow up with patients after they get treatment to make sure they come back in. It's a great way to counteract missed or broken appointments.

The same should go for reviews but, for some reason, there's a lapse in logic. While most of us proactively try to follow up with patients for treatment, many will fail to follow up with patients when it comes to reviews. Naturally, then, our patients will verbally promise to write us a review, only to end up forgetting.

Follow up your initial request for a review three days later with a reminder email containing links of where to submit reviews. Reminder emails can account for a huge percentage of review conversions.

## TIP 46

### Hang up a Sign in the Office

Many times, our patients aren't thinking of writing us a review even if they're getting high-quality care and genuinely love our practice. Hanging a sign in the office encouraging your patients to write a review on Google is a great way to remind them without asking them outright. It could simply be a sign that says, "If you had a great experience with us, write us a review on Google."

In my office, we use a sign that says "Got Gmail? Ask Us Why." It allows the patients to start the conversation when they do have a Gmail and want to inquire about the sign. From there, you can let them know that any patient with a Gmail email address or Google account can write a review on Google. You can now discuss how they can write the review with the patient because they have brought it up.

If you would like a copy of the sign I use, I would be happy to email it to you. Send a request to len@drlentau.com and I'll send it over.

# TIP 47

## Pro Tip: Reduce Friction

I'm always talking about creating a remarkable patient experience as key to your marketing success, and one concept you need to apply broadly is how many ways you can reduce friction in the patient experience. This changes the patient experience radically.

For example: Can they make and change appointments online? Can they fill out forms online ahead of time? Can they do financing chairside? Do you do teledentistry for your clear aligner clin-checks? Do you do single visit crowns using CAD/CAM? Make a concerted effort to apply this principle in as many aspects as possible, and watch the reviews and case acceptance go up!

—Fred Joyal, co-founder of 1-800-DENTIST

Fred Joyal is the co-founder of 1-800-DENTIST, and the bestselling author of Everything is Marketing, Becoming Remarkable and Superbold. He is a renowned speaker and business coach, and yet remains a terrible golfer.

# TIP 48

## Pro Tip: Trick or Treat?

As a general dentist, patients leave my office with a goodie bag. Inside the goodie bag, patients will find the usual stuff like a toothbrush, toothpaste, and floss. We know that patients will open this bag to get their goodies out, so we leverage that.

Attached to every toothbrush by a rubber band is a card reminding our patients to head over to Google to share their experiences. We make it easy for them by throwing a QR code and a customized, shortened, easy-to-type URL.

In case you want to see how that works, type bit.ly/jaadds3 in your browser. We find this subtle, easy reminder to be extremely effective when it comes to getting our existing patients to build our review numbers, all for free.

—Dr. Joshua Austin, Columnist at Dental Economics Magazine and Dentist at Joshua Austin DDS

Joshua Austin, DDS, MAGD, FACD, is a graduate of San Antonio's Health Careers High School, the University of Texas San Antonio, and the University of Texas Health Science Center San Antonio Dental School, one of the top-ranked dental schools in the nation since 1993. Dr. Austin excelled in dental school and was voted president of his graduating class. He capped off a successful senior year by being awarded the Texas Dental Association Outstanding Senior Dental Student award.

# TIP 49

## Create a QR Code Taking Them to Where They Can Write a Review

What is a QR code you ask? A QR code is short for "Quick Response" code. It's like a barcode, essentially, and it contains data for a locator, identifier, or tracker that points to a website or application.

When the Covid pandemic struck, QR codes rose to popularity, with many restaurants using them to share their menus with people instead of using physical menus.

In the context of this book, all you need to know is that a QR code offers a shortcut for patients to write a review. If you create a QR code, all your patients need to do is scan it with the camera or an app on their phone and it'll take them directly to a review site of your choice. You can put the QR code on many different things, such as signs in the office, social media, email signatures, and more.

This is what it could look like to use QR codes to get people to review your practice on a business card or sign.

HOW TO MAKE A DIFFERENCE IN YOUR OFFICE TODAY ★ 77

And here's a QR code that leads you to a page on my website where I feature several resources that help dental practices.

Finally, here's a picture from Dr. Katheryn Alderman of South Lincoln Family Dentistry, a dental practice that is using QR codes very effectively. Great job Katheryn.

> Your Next Appointment:
>
> ( Cancellations made with less than 48 business hours will result in a $75 cancellation fee. )
>
> Address:
> 2121 S. 70th Street, Lincoln, NE 68506
> Email:
> nebraskafamilydentistryslfd@gmail.com
> @southlincolnfamilydentistry
> @southlincolnfamilydentistry

Dr. Kathryn Alderman is not only a dentist, entrepreneur, mom, wife, teacher, mentor, and co-owner of many dental locations, she is also the CEO and founder of Progressive Practice Solutions. Progressive Practice Solutions helps practices focus on building people, optimizing services offered, and maximizing efficiency. You can learn more about Dr. Alderman and Progressive Practice Solutions at Linkedin.com/in/ProgressivePracticeSolutions.

# TIP 50

## Print Out a Prompt on Your Receipt

Another easy tip to implement in your office is to print out a prompt on the receipts for your patients. This is a great way to remind your patients that a review is very much appreciated.

When you give a patient a payment receipt, they might not even look at it. Perhaps they already know the cost or insurance has it covered. Just think about how often you look at receipts after you visit the doctor.

To make your prompt more noticeable, you should verbally ask them to write a review for you online and then show them the prompt on the receipt. This'll showcase to them that they have an easy way of going about it, and the instructions are readily available.

You can also use a QR code on the receipt to make it even easier for the patient.

## TIP 51

## Use a Printable Review Request Handout

Don't want to create a card or even a sign?

You can provide your patients a handout with visual instructions to write a review. Sometimes, all patients need is a reminder to leave you a review.

A handout is perfect. Hand it over to the patient after the appointment and explain that you'd love to hear their feedback. It can be in the form of a piece of paper attached to the invoice, a sticker, or even a few lines of text printed on your product packaging.

The important thing to remember is that your best patients are one step away from writing a great review of your business. Review request handouts are an effective tool to help you capitalize on this opportunity.

To see an example, visit the resources page at resources.drlentau.com.

# TIP 52

## Have Team Members Send Handwritten Notes

Handwritten notes don't just have to come from the doctor. Having a team member send a handwritten note can have a positive impact and generate a number of reviews, too.

Consider asking your hygienists to send follow-up notes after hygiene appointments to build rapport and loyalty. Print out cards that make it easy for your team members to write a short note and request a review, too.

Keep it simple. Even handwriting on a postcard with a QR code or short link to your reviews page that they send to your patient could help. They don't need to write a ten-page letter with a complete practice history. Even a few sentences does the trick.

# HOW TO UTILIZE ONLINE RESOURCES TO GET GREAT REVIEWS

★★★★★

# TIPS 53 – 58

## GENERAL TIPS

## TIP 53

### Ask for Patients for A Favor

If your patients have had a good experience with your dental office, they're usually more than happy to "pay it back" through a positive review. Framing your request as a "favor" lessens your patients' feeling of obligation. Interestingly enough, this makes them more likely to comply with your request.

Asking for a favor not only shows that you have trust in your patients, but it also allows them the opportunity to provide support for you and your office. When asked in the right way, most happy patients will be happy to leave a good review.

# TIP 54

## Share the Reviews You Received on Your Social Media Channels

I talk a lot about social proof and the "power of the crowd." When you see a lot of people doing something, oftentimes you'll follow. If you share your reviews from your patients on your social channels like Facebook, Twitter, and Instagram, it may convince other patients to talk about their experiences online as well.

More than anything, patients want a platform to express their feedback and feel they're being heard. Give them the space to do so by encouraging them to leave reviews.

One easy way to show users you're recognizing their contributions is to share their reviews on social media. You can either directly share their quote—while making sure to give them credit—or mock-up a nice-looking image to share.

# TIP 55

## Watch Their Memberships

People aren't likely to leave a review if they don't have an account on the review site of value. To find the optimum review platform to steer them to, you need to look for clues about where they've got accounts.

Did they reach out to you on Facebook? Asking for a Facebook recommendation becomes an easy choice. Email addresses can be a big clue, too. If they requested service with a Gmail address on your contact form, you know they can easily leave a Google review.

# TIP 56

## Shorten Your Review Shortcut

It's easy enough to drop your review shortcut link into a button on your website or hyperlink it through shorter anchor text on your website asking for feedback from patients.

Unfortunately, your full review shortcut link is a long eyesore that doesn't look nice outside of a button or hidden behind anchor text. Thankfully, there are free link shorteners out there like bitly.com through which you can shorten and even customize your review link. If your website is built on WordPress, you can use the free plugin Pretty Link Lite to create your own short links. The links could look like YourPractice.com/Google or YourPractice.com/Facebook. Other web builder platforms offer similar functionality, so ask your web developer what they can do to set that up for you.

Having a short, customized review link will be more appealing to patients. It will look cleaner and reassure your patients that you are the right choice for their needs.

# TIP 57

## Be Active in Responding to Reviews

I don't generally recommend responding to negative reviews online. I would rather you take it offline and contact the patient via email or phone and correct the issue directly. Many times they will take the review down or increase the star rating when you reach out personally.

You can respond to your positive reviews as long as you don't use the same automated response for every review you receive. That will make your practice look ingenuine and automated.

A recent study by Harvard Business Review offers some insight: Businesses begin to get 12% more reviews when they start responding to existing ones.[2] Responsiveness also leads to an increase in overall ratings by 0.12 stars.

If you do respond to a review, remember you are responding more to the people who are reading the review rather than the person who wrote the review. Be genuine and represent your practice well through your choice of words. Also, be conscious about avoiding a HIPAA violation. One piece of advice…Acknowledgment that they are a patient is considered a HIPAA violation.

---

[2] Davide Proserpio and Giorgos Zervas, "Study: Replying to Customer Reviews Results in Better Ratings," Harvard Business Review, February 14, 2018, https://hbr.org/2018/02/study-replying-to-customer-reviews-results-in-better-ratings.

# TIP 58

## Ensure Compliance

First off, it is important to identify the sites you are going to focus on and are allowed to incentivize feedback. Some sites such as Yelp frown upon businesses asking for reviews. You need to learn the terms of service for each of the review sites.

As you craft a strategy to get reviews, you want to be rewarded not penalized by asking for online reviews. As dentists, we know all about red tape. There are legal boundaries in the review world, too, and it's important not to step over any sidelines. Reviews are meant to make things easier for your dental practice, not cause you a headache.

Do your due diligence. You don't need to sift through a pile of contractual obligations, necessarily, but at least make sure you're not breaking any "big rules" that are made plain and clear.

# TIPS 59 – 63

## HOW TO USE EMAIL TO GENERATE REVIEWS

## TIP 59

## Run an Email Campaign to Get More Reviews

When a patient leaves the office, confirm the email you have on file for them in your practice management software. Don't forget to let them know that you are going to be sending them an email.

Keep the email concise, and when you write your message, be sure to include their name to make it more personal. Don't forget to add a link to the page where you'd like them to post a review. Just remember email open rates are not as high as they used to be as patients are bombarded by emails all day every day. How many unopened emails do you have in your inbox?

There's nothing wrong with trying to get a review from a patient who has not been in the practice for a year yet. Download a file of your patients from your practice management software and send an email to those that meet a certain qualification.

This can be specific patients who have had a certain procedure or who recently interacted with your practice.. By choosing a specific qualification, you can make your email more specific and relatable when sending to groups, large or small.

Regardless of the nature or size of your campaign, always remember to say thank you to your patients. Use your emails and messages as an opportunity to show appreciation for their feedback and encourage them to return to your practice. Since you are still sending an email the same rules apply as above: use their first name to make it more personal, keep the email concise, and add a link to the review page.

## TIP 60

### Make It Possible by Adding CTAs Where They Belong

It may seem obvious, but it's important. For your patients to leave reviews, you need to make it possible for them to write them! That means prominently featuring calls-to-action (CTA) for patients to leave a review.

You can leave CTAs on your website, at the end of every email, on your social media campaigns and posts, and more.

An example of a CTA could be: "Have feedback? Leave us a review on Google."

Adding a simple call to action like this in your default email signature or at the end of a social media post can generate a decent number of reviews on its own. Think about how many emails you send each month. Adding a link to your signature can be the easiest way to get a boost in your review count.

## TIP 61

## Include Reviews and Testimonials in Your Newsletters

You should include short reviews and testimonials in your newsletters and email communications. I rarely see emails these days that don't include testimonials and reviews.

Sharing your most powerful reviews with your prospective patients and existing patients on an ongoing basis builds their trust in you for when they come in for their next appointment.

This also plays into the social proof "power of the crowd" theory I mentioned earlier. If your patients see the other reviews, they will be more likely to leave one themselves. You can even include a link for patients to share their reviews and potentially be featured in a future newsletter.

# TIP 62

## Ask Individual Patients for Reviews via Email (With a Script)

Asking for reviews via email is a no-brainer and there are a couple of ways you can approach this.

Nothing can make a patient feel quite as appreciated as receiving a personal email from the business owner. Choose a handful of patients who have done a great deal of business with you, have recently completed a large case, or patients with whom you're hoping to cultivate lasting relationships and send them a personal note thanking them for their business and asking for the review.

Here is an example of what you can send them:

Dear [first name],

As one of our preferred patients, your feedback is of the utmost importance to [practice name]. We are constantly striving to provide the ideal experience for our patients, and your input helps us to define that experience. We would appreciate it if you could take a minute to post a review on [review platform].

We look forward to seeing you at your next appointment!

# TIP 63

## Email Blast Your Patients

Remember, text messaging is going to be a better option, especially for younger patients, but if you have an email list, you should use it to your advantage by emailing all of your patients from time to time. Depending on your software, you can exclude patients who have recently left a review by tagging them in your email software and then excluding people with those tags from your blast.

Here's a simple review request example you can use:

Good morning,

Positive reviews from awesome patients like you help others to feel confident about choosing [your practice name], too.

Could you take 60 seconds to go to [platform] and share your happy experiences?

We will be forever grateful. Thank you in advance for helping us out!

Here's a direct link to make it easier for you: [link to leave a review on the platform]

# TIPS 64 – 71

## HOW TO USE GOOGLE TO GENERATE REVIEWS

Leaving a Google review is a relatively quick and simple process. For the customer, it takes less than a minute of their day. For the business, the benefits are ongoing.

As a dental practice, you should always be trying to get more people to leave a Google review for your business. I'm not exaggerating when I say it's the key to accomplishing your short-term and long-term goals.

You might be thinking, why Google? There are so many places for your patients to leave reviews. That's true, but before you build upon your reputation on other platforms, you must first master Google. Google is the number one trusted site for business ratings and reviews. Establishing your practice on Google first will make using the other platforms much easier.

You can't build a house without a foundation. Likewise, if you don't have a good reputation on Google reviews, you won't have the foundation upon which to build the rest of your practice.

If you're not yet emphasizing Google business reviews, now's the time to change that. You ought to start prioritizing it in your local marketing strategy.

# TIP 64

## Get to Know Google's Policies

You must follow Google's Terms of Service when soliciting reviews. This means you should not offer any rewards to incentivize patients to leave a review.

Knowing Google's policies will ensure you won't be banned. It is important to familiarize yourself with the terms to prevent this. It's also important to do this for the sake of your practice, frankly.

If you're offering a poor customer experience or lackluster dentistry, persuading patients to give you reviews isn't something you should be focusing on. Improve your practice instead and you'll see honest feedback from genuinely happy patients. Reviews are just the cherry on top.

## TIP 65

## Make Sure Your Business is a "Place" on Google Maps

Ensuring your business is a "place" on Google Maps will give you a Google Business Profile on which customers can leave reviews. Not only will this make your practice seem more professional, but it'll also help people find your office with ease.

If it's hard for prospects to search for information about your office, it won't be worth the effort. They'll have an easier time going to a different practice with more apparent information on Google.

Fortunately, it's very simple to add your practice as a place. You can do it from any Android, computer, iPhone, or iPad. Get step-by-step instructions by visiting the resources page for this book at resources.drlentau.com or https://support.google.com/maps/answer/6320846.

## TIP 66

## Make Sure Your Google Business Profile is Verified

Creating a listing on Google Maps (which automatically creates a Business Profile) does not give you control over that listing. You need to create a Google Business Profile account and verify ownership of your Business Profile through that account. (Remember, as I mentioned in tip 22, Google renamed Google My Business to Google Business Profile in late 2021.)

By owning a Google Business Profile account, your patients will be able to find your information easier, your practice will appear more professional, and your business will rank higher on Google searches, making it easier for new patients to find you.

You need to show up on Google Maps when someone searches for your office. When you look at your Google Business Profile page does it say, "own this business?" If it does, you need to claim and verify your Google Business Profile page.

An unverified page will make people question the legitimacy of your practice. Make sure you get your page verified by Google to get the best results.

## TIP 67

## Create Your Own Google Review Link

As you know, you need to make it easy for your patients to write a review. An effective technique is to create your own Google review link.

This involves using the Google Business Profile API to create a link to a page where patients and Google users can review your business and share their experiences in your office.

Creating your own Google review link is crucial because it will allow you to respond to and manage the influx of reviews you'll be getting once you implement the tactics in this book.

If you need more help, use this link for Google's step-by-step instructions: https://support.google.com/business/answer/7035772

The Google review link is easy to place on your site, add to requests, or CTAs. Using this link is better than just linking to your Google page because patients won't have to try and find the review button, it will auto-open, they will choose stars, and then type.

## TIP 68

## Rank Positive Reviews as Helpful

On Google, you can give comments a boost by labeling them "helpful." Anyone can do this, but you can get a head start by labeling the most positive reviews as helpful.

Not only will this help you prioritize the most positive comments, which will help your business, but it will also show other users that people are reading the reviews—and can encourage them to jump in, too.

That said, don't just mark a review or comment as "helpful" simply because it was positive feedback. People will think something is fishy if a five-star review with a three-word endorsement wins out over a four-star review with thorough feedback and meticulous analysis.

## TIP 69

## Download the Google Maps App

The Google Maps app allows you to get your business on Google for free. When it comes to collecting Google reviews, this app is super helpful.

If you put the Google Maps app on your phone it makes it easy to email or text a patient to ask for a review. It can take your patient right to your listing to leave a review.

## TIP 70

## Use the Google Business Profile Marketing Kit

The Google Business Profile Marketing Kit website lets you create, download, and print personalized marketing materials that help convince patients to leave a review after they purchase.

Assets include social posts, stickers, and other pieces of collateral to promote your business online and offline.

You can even take it one step further and customize each asset to comply with your brand guidelines.

To get this free toolkit visit https://marketingkit.withgoogle.com/

## TIP 71

## Promote Your Reviews in A Paid Ad

What better way to earn trust than to promote your reputation in a paid advertisement? Instead of advertising a product or service you provide such as veneers or Invisalign, promote your business' reputation!

Since reputation impacts a patient's buying process, seeing positive reviews or five yellow stars associated with your dental office helps build credibility and can nudge potential patients to contact you instead of a competitor.

# TIPS 72 – 78

## HOW TO USE FACEBOOK TO GENERATE REVIEWS

In the Spring of 2018, Facebook started improving the way reviews are left on business pages. In the past, a review would consist of a paragraph explaining a person's experience along with their rating.

Facebook reviews should be very high on your list, a notch below Google reviews. When doing a Google search for your office, they will be able to see the number of reviews and the star rating within that Google search. To add to this, many people look up businesses on Facebook to check out reviews, recommendations, social proof, and to "get to know" the practice.

# TIP 72

## Make Sure Your Review Tab Is Visible

If you go on the Facebook page of a few of your favorite businesses, you may notice that you are not able to leave a review for them because they don't have that feature activated.

Many businesses don't even realize they have this feature turned off.

Facebook has evolved its review system and simplified it over time. The process is initiated with a simple question: "Do you recommend this place?"

To turn Recommendations on or off for your Page:

1. From your News Feed, click Pages in the left menu.
2. Go to your Page.
3. Click Page Settings in the bottom left of your Page.
4. Click Templates and Tabs in the left menu.
5. Click to the right of Reviews to turn the tab on or off.

Note: If your Page previously had reviews, your recommendations might have been automatically turned on for your Page. If you can't find a review, check your Page's reviews and recommendations (you can filter by most recent recommendations to help you find them). If you still can't find a review or recommendation, it may have been removed because it didn't follow Facebook's community standards.

Activating your Facebook reviews is a major help when it comes to boosting your total review numbers and ratings.

## TIP 73

### Create a Check-in Offer

Checking in on Facebook is simple and fun for customers to brag to their Facebook friends where they are.

This also sometimes leads to Facebook sending a reminder for the user's recommendation after leaving.

Create some incentives for people to check-in like access to a WiFi password, a free upgrade, free teeth whitening, a gift card, or a small discount for checking into your Facebook page.

Be creative, you can offer anything of value.

## TIP 74

## Respond to Reviews on Facebook

Social media is all about having a conversation online, so you need to be listening to your patients. And, on Facebook and other social media websites, people expect responses. That's why it's even more important to respond on Facebook than many other review sites. Most of the time when our patients are interacting with us online it's because they want to be heard.

If someone takes the time to review you, give them the decency of a response, even if it is negative, and take time to address their concerns. Of course, be careful not to violate HIPAA or engage in a public back-and-forth. You could simply reply to a negative post by thanking them for taking the time to share their review and let them know someone will be in touch to help address their concerns.

You could also reach out before replying to a negative review, which is my preferred method. You may just turn them into your biggest fan by listening and acknowledging them. When you do, patients often update or delete their negative review.

# TIP 75

## Promote Reviews on Facebook

Get your favorite reviews seen by thousands of prospective patients by promoting them on Facebook. Take some of your best reviews, add a great visual, and then show them off to Facebook users.

You only need to spend $5 to $20 promoting it to get your positive reviews in front of hundreds or even thousands of potential patients. When other people see your great feedback, they will be more interested in becoming your patient.

## TIP 76

## Include Facebook Buttons in Follow-Ups With Patients via Email or Text

Facebook is constantly coming out with new features, and it can be hard to keep up with everything. If you haven't heard of Facebook Buttons, they're calls to action. They give people an easy way for recipients of your message to respond and take action.

Anytime you are responding to a comment or following up after a patient's visit, you should be including Facebook buttons. Attaching a Facebook button within the message will help guide your patients to the right place and easily write a review.

## TIP 77

## Pro Tip: Get Involved with Instagram

Instagram is another social media platform that can help you grow your practice. Patients love to be able to see who you really are, what your practice looks like, how you treat your team, and how happy your patients are. It only makes sense we would want to share our best reviews on this social page.

Instagram is a visual platform that favors video content. If you can capture your patient sharing their smile reveal, expressing how much they love and appreciate your work, or any positive experience working with you or your team, then you're going to have one very powerful review! You can ask your patients if you can tag them using their Instagram handle (the name that starts with the @ sign). When you do that, and the patient shares the video or the clip onto their Instagram page, all their friends and family will get to see the office Instagram and how happy the patient was to be there. This creates a powerful digital internal referral system that can act as a platform to get your office name and page in front of so many more people in a genuine way—for free!

Your patients are looking for social proof—real people that had real results. This allows your patient to walk into your practice already knowing you, liking you, and trusting you. The benefits of this are huge because your patient comes in with more knowledge of who you are and the amazing work that you do, even before they speak to you. This can increase case conversion, improve procedure education, and even have your patients ask about specific procedures like whitening or Invisalign.

> "Very friendly experience for the first visit. I think I found my new favorite place 😁."
>
> Google Review
> 6/19/20
> By Alex A.

If you are not able to get a video testimonial, or you feel that is not the right fit for your practice, then at the very least, take the reviews you are getting from Google and create an image using Canva or another digital creation website and create a 1080 x 1080 square post with your logo and branded colors. Post the newly designed Google review to your Instagram weekly so your patients and potential patients get to see just how happy your patients are coming to you!

—Allison Lacoursiere

Allison Lacoursiere helps dental professionals streamline efficiencies to increase both patient and practice satisfaction and health. Learn how to develop a wider patient base, boost team engagement, optimize systems, and leverage Instagram to improve patient lives and the practice bottom line by visiting YourClearAlignerCoach.com.

## TIP 78

## Using Your Patients Voice on Social Channels

Sharing third-party validation on social media helps increase your brand's credibility, can boost engagement, and grow your office's bottom line.

To demonstrate, here is an example of how I promoted implants and a patient experience by highlighting a review we received.

As you can see, the text and image of the advertisement included the patient review and the call-to-action on the advertisement was to book a free dental implant consultation.

> **Pennsylvania Center for Dental Excellence**
> Sponsored
>
> "Everyone was very friendly and helpful! Dr. Tau took his time and explained all my options so that I was able to make and informed choice.
> I'm glad that I decide to go to this office. I would definitely recommend them!"
> - Yvette Law
>
> " Dr. Tau took his time and explained all my options so that I was able to make and informed choice"
> - Yvette L.
>
> PENNSYLVANIA CENTER
> *Dental Excellence*
> Leonard F. Tau, DMD
>
> HTTPS://INFO.PHILADELPHIAPA.DENTIST/APPLY-FOR-A-FR...
> **Book a Free Dental Implant Consultation with One of Top Dentists in Philadelphia**
> Learn More

# TIPS 79 – 84

## HOW TO USE YELP TO GENERATE REVIEWS

Yelp is possibly the most restrictive of all the business directories and reviews sites when it comes to asking for patient reviews. "Asking" for a review is forbidden, according to its policy guidelines.

Here are the specific guidelines regarding how to get Yelp reviews:

- Do not ask for Yelp reviews—this includes not asking patients, family, friends, or anyone else.
- Do not have competitions for your team to collect reviews.
- Don't use surveys to request reviews from patients who report positive experiences.
- Don't run any type of promotions including discounts, payments, or giveaways in exchange for Yelp reviews.

Yelp defends its policy by saying that review solicitation could lead to mistrust due to the likelihood that businesses would only encourage positive reviews,

They want the reviews to be organic. In the following tips, I'll share the best ways to get reviews on Yelp.

# TIP 79

## Identify Yelpers in Your Practice

The first beneficial step is to identify your patients who use Yelp. Yelp has an algorithm that many times will only keep reviews from frequent users of Yelp from being placed in the "not recommended" section of the reviews.

If you can identify those patients who are Yelpers, the reviews they leave you are most likely to stick. Use a sign in the office asking if they are a Yelper. The sign can say something to the effect of, "Are you a Yelper? Let us know."

Once your patients see the sign and say that they are, that is the perfect opportunity to ask if they would like to write a review for your practice. Be sure to not specifically ask for Yelp reviews when you ask to avoid violating Yelp's rule to not ask specifically for Yelp reviews. But if you have a card with all the options to review you, including Yelp, hand them that to let them know their options. You will have planted a seed in their brain to leave a Yelp review and that's the best you can do. Because they are Yelpers, these reviews should remain in the recommended section.

# TIP 80

## Create a Yelp Check-In Offer

As I stated above, the reviews that matter to Yelp are ones from their trusted and frequent users. When frequent users use any business, they are known to want to check-in to let everyone know they are at the place of business.

If you create a check-in offer, a free whitening pen, a discount on treatment, not only is it instant word-of-mouth advertising, but it alerts Yelp that the patient is physically in your office.

Later that day or the next day Yelp will send that patient a review request of their own. You want to use breadcrumbs to get the patients to write a review, as Yelp wants them to be organic.

To download an example of a Yelp check in flyer check out the book resources page at resources.drlentau.com.

## TIP 81

### Give Your Patients a "Heads-Up"

Instead of saying "Write a review about our business on Yelp," say, "Check us out on Yelp."

The first is a solicitation while the latter is a "heads up," an FYI that raises awareness.

The difference may be slight, but it's worth noting and it is within Yelp's Terms and Conditions to be able to do this.

A little change in your language can result in big results online; changing from asking for a review to asking for feedback.

# TIP 82

## Put a Badge on Your Website

Some folks like to spice things up with decorations whether it's their car, laptop, bedroom wall, or living room. For a business, you can spice things up on Yelp with digital "Review Badges."

Review Badges allow practices to showcase their Yelp reviews on their website. This is a good way to showcase Yelp as an option for patients to review your practice.

Yelp offers several designs that you can put on your site, which link to your business profile. Just copy and paste the HTML code associated with each badge into the site. Review averages and counts update automatically as new reviews come in.

## TIP 83

### Claim Your Yelp Listing

Many offices are put off by Yelp because of their business practices, but Yelp is an incredibly important citation and must be claimed to help with local ranking.

Google has great trust with Yelp. Claiming your business is a way of stating you're authorized to speak for it.

To make this step, visit Yelp's Find and Claim page and search for your business.

Once you've successfully claimed the business, you can respond to reviews and activity on the page.

## TIP 84

## Optimize Your Yelp Page

You should optimize your Yelp page by adding all relevant information about your business, such as hours and parking information.

Upload high-quality photos of your location, doctor, team, and even before-and-after smiles.

Photos are really important to Yelp. In fact, users spend 2.5 times longer looking at pages that include photos than those without photos.

They also come off as more authentic than a simple text review.

# TIPS 85 – 94

## HOW TO USE YOUTUBE TO GENERATE REVIEWS

I have renamed YouTube testimonials as "Trustamonials," as they help create trust between your business and the patient.

If you don't have a YouTube channel for your dental practice, you may want to consider it as another outlet for marketing your practice online.

Your YouTube videos can send a great deal of traffic to your website from people who find them when searching YouTube or Google for a local dentist online.

You may be wondering what kind of content a dentist can post on YouTube, but the opportunities are endless. Think about what someone might want to know about dentistry, or what you are passionate about, and make videos on it.

# TIP 85

## Ask Your Super Happy Patients to Provide a Video Testimonial

There is something about watching and listening to someone talk about their experiences in your office rather than just reading about it. Video is such a powerful tool we have now with everyone having a smartphone.

After you finish a procedure, such as Invisalign or a smile makeover, ask them if they are comfortable doing a video. If they are, you are golden. Capture the unveiling of the new smile, their reaction, their experience. Let them tell their story. It's magic.

In today's digital age, it's easy to question whether online reviews and testimonials are authentic. However, no one can question the veracity of a video review. It also creates the opportunity to include the emotion of the audio message, which cannot be conveyed via images and text. Remember, buyers make emotional decisions followed by logical reasoning to support their decisions.

Every office should invest in a video recorder. I use my iPhone and an Osmo 2, which is a Gimbal or Steadicam so you can quickly capture those magic words on the spot. Remember to have the patient sign a HIPAA release in order to post to Facebook and YouTube.

# TIP 86

## Use Your Smartphone to Record

There's no need for high-end video cameras. If anything, they'll probably make your patients nervous.

You don't want them thinking they're on some reality show or that you're a bigwig who sees them as a number. Keep it casual.

Use your iPhone or Android since it is easy to access in your pocket. Nowadays our smartphones have high-quality cameras and audio anyways, and your patient doesn't need to get overwhelmed by a high-end video camera. It will make the video less genuine and believable.

# TIP 87

## Use a Gimbal or Steadicam

You're not a professional filmmaker; you're a dentist. I don't care if you think the aesthetic of a shakier handheld camera makes it look more authentic. Let's stay in our lane and let Spielberg take care of the fancier stuff.

We're dentists, and dentistry requires steady hands. Yet, somehow, most of us find it hard to hold a camera steady. If that sounds like you, you can use one of these devices to prevent SCS (shaky camera syndrome). A great solution is a Gimbal or Steadicam. Just go with whatever is in your budget; there's no need to spend thousands.

## TIP 88

## Make Sure You Film in a Quiet Area

What do they say at the movies? Ah, that's right… "Silence is golden."

When it comes to filming any testimonials from patients, that saying goes more than ever. You don't need to set up studio lights and give them a script, but you can at least reduce background noise. Otherwise, any external sounds are going to distract from whatever your patient is saying and maybe even disrupt their train of thought.

Do you have a private space in your office? Maybe you have a consultation room or private office that you can use to record. It is best to film with as little background noise as possible. It makes hearing the patient and what they have to say much easier and makes the video much more professional.

## TIP 89

## Keep the Videos Short

Fast-paced videos dominate the web for a reason. People have short attention spans, and anything that's going to take more than a minute is likely to be scrolled past.

Keep the videos short to keep them snackable and you'll be much more likely to stop people mid-scroll.

It is best to keep these videos concise. You should aim for around 30 to 60 seconds, maximum, as people who are watching will have a limited attention span.

No one wants to watch a five-minute long review video when it can easily be cut shorter.

# TIP 90

## Coach the Patients on What They Should Say

Sometimes it's best to lay out the foundation of the review so that they hit the main points and don't get off-topic. Don't put words in their mouth but key information like your practice name and the experience they had need to be brought up.

It's not about providing a script or getting an inauthentic review. The idea is to have your patients say what will be relevant for a review. If you give them a framework by asking specific questions or coaching them on what they should focus on, it'll make it smoother sailing for both parties—you'll get a good review and they'll be able to finish faster.

# TIP 91

## First Take Is Usually the Best

If you're like most people, you've probably had to sit in front of a camera and put on a forced smile. And you probably have noticed that forceful smiles aren't nearly as good as authentic, candid smiles. It's the reason why people always crack a joke before the picture, after all.

The same goes with filming a patient who is giving a review.

Try not to overproduce or film the video too many times to keep the video genuine.

Unless the patient flubs the lines, capturing the raw footage is the very best way to create trust with the viewer.

## TIP 92

## Have a Release Ready

Notice how they often blur out faces on reality TV? That's because you can't just film anybody and put it out for the world to see.

You need permission from the person who is being filmed, otherwise, you'll be running into some legal violations.

You ought to be asking the patient ahead of time whether they're comfortable with you filming them.

Don't beat around the bush, either. Let them know that you want to use it on YouTube and other social media channels such as Facebook, Instagram, and your website.

Make sure you get a HIPAA release signed giving you explicit permission to use the videos.

## TIP 93

### Set up a YouTube Channel

Getting started on YouTube is easy. Just a few simple steps and you're ready to dive into the second most used search engine.

You can sign into YouTube using the Google account that you used to create your business's Google Local listing.

Your new YouTube channel will have the same name as your Google Business Profile and these accounts will be connected, making it simple to keep track of and update these accounts.

## TIP 94

### Upload Your Videos

Now, upload your first video! Click "Upload" at the top of the page and upload the video from your computer.

Give it a good descriptive title, "tag" it with descriptive keywords, and write a description to go along with it. Voila, you are done.

From there, you can embed the video in multiple places.

YouTube provides you with coding that you can use to put the YouTube video you uploaded to your website, Facebook, and other social media channels.

Share your videos on your website and social platforms.

# TIPS 95 – 98

## HOW TO USE LINKEDIN TO GENERATE REVIEWS

# TIP 95

## Trade Recommendations with Coworkers/Employees

If you're running a dental practice, you have employees and coworkers. See if they'd be willing to trade LinkedIn reviews, benefiting both of you.

Ultimately, if you (or the office you work for) has employees listed under the company page and multiple employees have great recommendations, this benefits everyone involved.

Sometimes, seeing a review on your profile can be enough to let your clients know they can leave one, too.

Some people either forget about this option on LinkedIn or they don't even know about it at all.

# TIP 96

## Place Best Recommendations Higher Up

Putting the most detailed, most positive recommendations first will encourage other clients to leave you reviews to follow suit.

When it comes to LinkedIn, it's all about the details, and everyone likes to have an idea of what they should say.

It's much easier for your patients to leave reviews when they see other people's reviews because it gives them a basis for where to start.

# TIP 97

## Invite Connections to Review You

While you can (and should) ask for reviews off-platform, you can also invite connections to write you a recommendation on LinkedIn. They'll get an email and a notification, and it's almost more work for them to ignore the message than to just write the recommendation.

You don't want to spam every new connection, though. If some financial advisor from Oregon connects with you, for example, and you're located in Texas, then there's no reason to ask that person for a review. They've never been to your practice and probably never will.

Pick and choose between who is relevant.

## TIP 98

## Promote Your Profiles on Your Site and Email

Some multiple plugins and tools let you promote your LinkedIn on your website and email.

Since LinkedIn doesn't get as much traffic as other profiles might, just getting more connections can mean more reviews.

Now that I covered other platforms, you can begin to use them to get more reviews and grow your practice.

The next step is knowing what to avoid so you don't end up digging yourself a hole.

(I'll share tips on what to avoid later in the book.)

# TIPS 99 – 102

## HOW TO USE YOUR WEBSITE TO GENERATE REVIEWS

## TIP 99

## Have More Than One Page or Place on Your Website for Reviews or Testimonials

Feature testimonials and reviews on every single page of your website, especially on your "smile gallery" where you feature your patients. Positioning them near the primary call-to-action area of the page increases the likelihood of getting your visitors to take your desired action.

For example, if you are offering a gift or special offer on your home page, you can put one or two powerful testimonials adjacent to the submit button that are relevant to your offer. This will make it easier to promote what you are offering and intrigue patients to leave their own reviews at the same time.

# TIP 100

## Link to Your Google Review Page From Your Website

If a customer wants to leave a review for your business, the first place they're probably going to look is your website. That's why you should provide a clear and clutter-free call-to-action that is intuitively easy to find.

You should make the CTA button visible on the website before the user even has to scroll. This will help generate more leads that can convert into reviews for your practice.

When an existing patient is on your website you want to make it easy for them to write a review for you.

Add a button that says, "write a review" or "see what others say about our office."

Feature some testimonials from your existing patients and make it easy for them to leave a review for you as well.

Make sure the button is easily seen on the home page.

On my practice's website, we call that page "Raving Patients," but you can call it "Patient Reviews" or "Patient Testimonials."

## TIP 101

## Create a Google Reviews Page on Your Website

In addition to a button, you could also dedicate a full website page to Google reviews (or reviews in general), accessible from your main navigation menu.

The page should contain both a CTA to write a review but also include existing reviews. These not only encourage prospects to become patients but also give that added inspiration for an existing patient to leave a review.

You can populate your reviews page via screenshots. Many practices do. Ideally, you would want to add the text from the review as well. The reason for this is that reviews are often keyword-rich, so including them on your website in a way that Google's crawlers can "read" makes for a great small business SEO strategy.

You can come up with a template where you can copy and paste the text in. Some platforms and plug-ins allow you to aggregate your Google reviews onto your website automatically.

If you or your web developer need help setting this up, visit the resources page at resources.drlentau.com.

# TIP 102

## Pro Tip: Don't be Afraid to Recycle Reviews for Content

Don't be afraid to recycle reviews for content. One of my favorite things to do is to use screenshots of reviews from Google. The Google format of review has become very recognizable, and using a screenshot gives instant credibility.

It has been shown to be very effective, and even more effective than just copying the text. Use these screenshots overlaid on your branding or photos. Put it on your website interspersed among text. Put them everywhere that you can!

—Jason Lipscomb

Jason Lipscomb is a general dentist in Richmond, VA. Dr. Lipscomb has two practices and enjoys operating the Dental Disrupt Nation Facebook page. He has been a dental speaker on digital marketing since 2008 and loves a good dental meme.

# TIPS 103 – 109

## HOW TO USE SOFTWARE TO GENERATE REVIEWS

# TIP 103

## Pro Tip: Set-It-And-Forget-It

Like many aspects of dentistry today, automation can drastically improve the number of reviews you get in your office.

Relying on team members who already have too much on their plate to also ask for reviews will not accomplish the goals most are looking for.

Using a software platform that allows you to automate your review collection process and truly "set-it-and-forget-it" is the pathway to maximize the number of reviews you get.

—Bryan Laskin, DDS, Lake Minnetonka Dental

Dr. Laskin is passionate about improving lives by elevating health through teamwork and technology. He believes that by offering patients same-day convenience while providing care "at your pace" is one way to achieve this. He has been recognized by his peers, voted a "Top Dentist" in both *Minneapolis/St. Paul* and *Minnesota Monthly* magazines. Learn more about Dr. Laskin at LakeMinnetonkaDental.com.

# TIP 104

## Utilize Reputation Marketing Software

While I am biased toward using Google as your prioritized review platform, there are marketing software programs that can help request reviews on Google and other platforms. For example, Birdeye is an automated reputation marketing platform that sends a text message to your patients after their appointment. It's the one I use and recommend, as I'm the head of their dental vertical.

Birdeye is integrated with 98% of practice management software programs so you can just send text messages through your software to request feedback and let Birdeye take care of the rest. The text message asks for feedback about their experience in the office. When they click on the link, they are taken on the Android phone directly to Google or on the iPhone given a choice of Google or Facebook.

The review is cross-posted to your business Facebook page and website. It is super simple and easy for the patient to use. Patients don't get annoyed since we only send the text message one time in 30 days. The best part is once it is set up, your team does not have to do anything—which they love.

**Birdeye** — To find out more about what Birdeye can do for your office, request a demo at drlentau.as.me/birdeye.

## TIP 105

## Use Text Messaging Software

Using an automated service to send out a text message is probably the most effective way to have a patient leave a review. That's why reputation marketing software like Birdeye helps you automate the entire process.

If you do not want to use an automated service, you can choose to send out a text either manually or through text messaging software, such as SlickText to ask the patient for a review after they leave the appointment. It won't be as automated or walk them through the entire process, even if you use text messaging software, but it will get the patient's attention better than email many times.

Just send them a request and the Google review link you created by taking action on another tip. The toughest part about this is remaining consistent in sending out the messages to your patients and following up without the automated reminders you can send out using reputation marketing software like Birdeye.

# TIP 106

## Create a Points System

Some patient communication software, such as Modento, which I use and recommend highly to anyone looking for a new communication software, allows you to use a point system to encourage and reward patients for doing things like filling out forms, showing up on time, downloading an app, and more.

Add a review to the list of things they receive points for, which they can later turn in for a prize.

This is a great way to encourage your patients to engage more with your practice all while getting more reviews.

Modesto has so many additional features, such as online scheduling, collecting digital forms, virtual appointment check-ins, and collecting online payments. Modesto has also generously offered readers of this book savings on their setup fees. To find out more about Modesto, schedule a demo, and save on setup fees use this link: https://info.modento.io/lentau.

## TIP 107

## Use a WordPress Business Review Widget

While there are plenty of generic review widgets available, WordPress Review Widgets are built specifically to work with WordPress websites.

Not only are these widgets easy to use within your existing WordPress dashboard, but they also offer a superior user experience that allows you to directly integrate Google reviews.

This is an easy tool to implement, especially if you are already familiar with WordPress. You can directly integrate your Google reviews to your practice's website with no challenge.

## TIP 108

## Use Your Office WiFi to Get Reviews From Your Patients

A company like Social WiFi can help your patients use the power of the WiFi that you have in your office to do things like liking your Facebook page, checking-in at your office, or leaving a review.

Social WiFi will send a review request email to each WiFi user to evaluate their experience, but as always it is sent with your branding.

Check out SocialWifi.com for more information.

## TIP 109

## Pro Tip: Mindsight

"Mindsight" prevents practices from engaging in the right type of behavior to go out and get reviews. There's a fear that you'll get bad reviews and that your staff won't go out and ask for reviews.

Engaging your patients properly is the key.

1. Leverage software so you don't have to ask every single patient for a review.

Your staff isn't going to want to ask every single patient. You need consistency over time.

2. Engage patients in a way that is the most convenient for them.

Ask your patients to fill out a survey asking what review method they prefer. This could be through texts, email, or in person.

3. Send the survey out immediately before they leave the practice.

This is helpful because the patient is likely still in a good mood and their attention is still on your practice and not their daily lives.

4. Have the staff remind your patients on the way out to fill out the reviews.

—Adam Zilko, CEO & founder of
Firegang Dental Marketing

Adam Zilko provides a cutting edge, competitive, and highly effective approach to dominating local online markets. Adam's powerful, fully-integrated marketing method is encapsulated in his bestselling book, *Practice Growth for the Future-Focused Dentist*.

# TIPS 110 – 125

## HOW TO AVOID COMMON MISTAKES

## TIP 110

## Don't Incentivize Patients

It is against the terms and conditions of most review sites to offer an incentive for an online review.

Whether it be a five-dollar Starbucks gift card or a $30 credit to their account, you do not want to be doing this.

Elite Yelpers are incentivized to let Yelp know about this. Also, your competitors can report you and you can lose not some but all of the reviews you generated.

Don't take the risk to gain a few reviews and end up losing the ones you already have.

# TIP 111

## Don't Buy Reviews

Don't even think about this.

There are unscrupulous companies on the internet claiming that they can either write online reviews for you or get them for you. You need to handle this internally. There is no shortcut to online review generation, it takes time.

While it may be a little frustrating, it pays huge dividends once you hit a certain threshold. Are you that desperate for recognition or accolades? Positive word of mouth comes organically from your patients.

## TIP 112

## Don't Set Up a Review Kiosk in Your Office

A tablet or computer that collects reviews is against the terms and conditions of most, if not all, reviews sites now. If you do this, your reviews will come from one IP address and will alert the sites that you are trying to manipulate the system.

Patients should ideally be doing the reviews outside the office after their appointment. If they're coming back for a follow-up appointment, sitting in your lobby, waiting for treatment, and they've just remembered to leave you a review, that's different—that happened on their prerogative.

For the most part, however, reviews are happening once a patient has left your office—no if's, and's, or but's.

# TIP 113

## Don't Write Angry Rebuttals to a Negative Review

I always say it is best to take a deep breath and relax after you receive a negative review.

Does it hurt? Yes.

Is it the end of the world? No.

The best defense against negative reviews is more positive reviews.

If you are angry when you respond, you may regret the response you leave and it may have long-term ramifications on your practice.

## TIP 114

## Pro Tip: The Best Way to Handle a Negative Review

Remember, even though we live in a high-tech world where we have come to expect texts, voicemails, and other forms of communication to be met with near instant replies, it is always best to allow yourself to cool down before responding to a negative review.

Personally, I usually wait a day to formulate my response. This is particularly important when the scathing review is unwarranted, unfair, or even an outright lie. When responding, remember that your message should be targeted to the people *reading* your response, not to the person who left the review.

Responding to negative reviews should be viewed as an opportunity to showcase your practice and your professionalism. It should never be done to leave the response that "feels good."

Leave those "feel good comments" for complaining to your friends in dentist-only Facebook groups!

—Doc Hoffpauir

Doc Hoffpauir two dental practices in Texas and is part-owner of several other companies: Straight Teeth Solutions, a clear aligner company; Dentalogic, a medical and dental information services company; 4G Dental Laboratory; Dream Makers Industries, a small business incubator; nfoldAI, Inc., an artificial intelligence company; Doc Hoff Investments; and Still Waters Brazilian Jiu Jitsu Academy.

He maintains a strong online presence with his podcast, "Dear Doc," and he owns and moderates the largest social media page for dentists called "The Business of Dentistry." His newest venture is a new podcast called "Riveted, The Extraordinary Lives of Ordinary Folks."

## TIP 115

### Don't Just Give Up

Receiving negative reviews does not mean giving up on building your reviews. I have been vocal about advocating for not responding online to a negative review, but I certainly do not want you to completely ignore it, either.

You should try to contact the patient offline to try and correct the problem. A little goodwill goes a long way.

When you take the time to personally connect with the patient who left the bad review, it shows you care and are looking to improve. Many times, you will learn that the patient just needed to be heard and the solution is more reasonable than you think. Very frequently, the patient will even take down their review or increase their rating.

# TIP 116

## Don't Wait

It takes time to populate the web with positive content which minimizes the impact of potential future negative content.

The worst thing you can do is to wait to get started. The sooner you begin implementing these strategies, the faster you'll get positive reviews for your practice.

That said, don't rush into things. It's better to act, but make sure the action you're taking is structured with a clear-cut objective or general plan.

I've learned from trial and error that trying to do everything with blinders on can lead to a lot of missed opportunities.

# TIP 117

## Don't Threaten Legal Action or Sue a Patient for a Bad Review

Have you ever heard of the Streisand Effect?

The Streisand Effect is a social phenomenon that occurs when someone tries to hide negative information, but instead this action has the unintentional repercussion of distributing the information even further.

It comes from an attempt by Barbara Streisand to have a picture of her house removed from a collection of images used to document coastal erosion in California. Streisand sued a photographer and website for violating her privacy rights.[3]

Before she filed the lawsuit, the court noted that the image had only been downloaded six times, two of which were by her lawyer. In the first month after filing the lawsuit, however, more than 420,000 people visited the website. Not only did Streisand end up getting significantly more attention to the image than had she left the image alone, she ended up losing the lawsuit and having to pay the defendant $155,567.04 in legal fees.[4]

---

[3] Paul Rogers, "Welcome to the Mercury News on Bayarea.com," www.californiacoastline.org, June 24, 2003, https://www.californiacoastline.org/news/sjmerc5.html.

[4] "California Coastal Records Project," www.californiacoastline.org, accessed November 24, 2021, https://www.californiacoastline.org/streisand/lawsuit.html.

Nothing good will come from threatening legal action or suing a patient for a bad review. You will only attract negative press and it will hurt you in more ways than you know.

It's best to either let negative reviews roll off your shoulder or directly address it and try to fix it.

## TIP 118

## Don't Pay a Reputation Management Company to Get Negative Reviews off the First Page

Reputation management is an old term. Reverse SEO uses the power of your happy patients to get more positives to overwhelm the negatives. If you pay a reputation management company, you will pay a lot of money with no guarantees.

To add to that, the negative reviews will make your office look more credible online. If somebody has tons of five-star reviews and nothing in between, that's fishy. No business—dental practice or not—makes everyone into a raving fan. That's not realistic, with or without the "trolls" prowling through the online space.

## TIP 119

### Don't Enter Into a War of Words

The worst thing a business can do is to let a review site become a forum for arguing.

If you feel a patient has been unfair or is very unhappy, don't start to defend everything about your business there and then.

Your response should be short, friendly, and practical.

If possible, try to resolve their complaint by directing the patient to another channel (email, phone, etc.) where you can discuss the matter one-on-one.

If you handle it well, they may even end up leaving a good review.

## TIP 120

### Don't "Own" the Reviews

Some companies have your patients sign over copyright on anything written online about the practice.

In the past, this has led to offices running into major problems since they have used this form to try and get patients to remove online reviews. Do not use this type of form to control your reputation.

Forcing patients to sign away the copyrights to their reviews is off-putting, to say the least.

Nobody wants to feel like they just agreed to something they're not even sure about, and a review isn't worth that uncertainty for the vast majority of people.

## TIP 121

# Don't Copy Reviews From Another Office and Use Them for Yourself

Notice anything strange about these images?

**Jacky M.**
Southlake, TX
0 friends
2 reviews

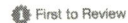

★★★★★ 11/20/2015
First to Review

What a feel good place! ...and that's usually hard to say about a dentistry...
Dr. Al did a great job in putting my little girl at ease at her very first dental visit. Our whole family is going there. The place feels like a spa with top notch equipment and wonderful professional staff. Love it!

Was this review ...?

Useful    Funny    Cool

---

"I had an appointment with Dr. Al a week ago. I must say my experience was wonderful and very professional from the beginning until the end. The team and especially Dr. Al took care of me how non other dentist did before, the commitment to his job is extraordinary. He explained to me in detail, step by step everything about the procedures so I could be calm during the intervention. Also, they offer extra features to make much more confortable your time there: Massage chair, warm blankets, pillows, etc I felt in very good hands. Definitely it was beyond my expectations and I'll be back with no doubt. Love this place!! Thank you Dr. Al!!!"

Elisabet P

"What a feel good place! ...and that's usually hard to say about a dentistry...
Dr. Al did a great job in putting my little girl at ease at her very first dental visit. Our whole family is going there. The place feels like a spa with top notch equipment and wonderful professional staff. Love it!"

Jacky M.

> "What a feel good place! ...and that's usually hard to say about a dentistry... SDG did a great job in putting my little girl at ease at her very first dental visit. Our whole family is going there. The place feels like a spa with top notch equipment and wonderful professional staff. Love it!"
>
> **Joseph Smith**
> Businessman

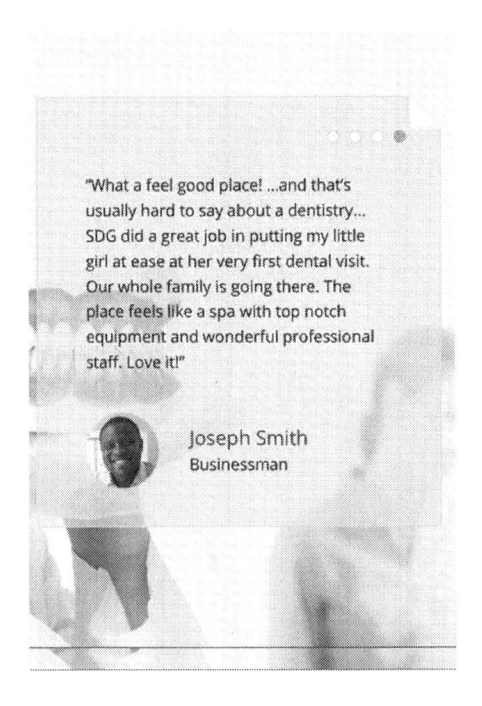

Yes, it looks like one practice got a review on Yelp and shared it on their website. Then, another practice copied the review from the first practice, changed the name of the reviewer, and used it on their website.

Not only is this a big reputation risk because it's only a matter of time before someone discovers it, but it can also present a legal risk. Using unfair or deceptive acts or practices to promote your practice isn't looked upon very fondly by the Federal Trade Commission and they *do* go after people for it.

Yes, you might get away with it for a little while, but you risk legal and reputational consequences if you get caught. It's already so easy to earn and collect a steady stream of real, positive reviews, it's not worth the risk.

# TIP 122

## Don't Use a Service That "Proxy Posts" Your Reviews to Multiple Sites

These reviews are collected in the office and then appear on other sites (not from the patient).

This is a process that is considered a "black hat" and can cause considerable problems for you online.

To legitimately get reviews on the sites that matter, they must be placed by the patient, not by service.

You can't buy reviews like you'd buy followers on Instagram or Twitter.

It needs to be a very organic process, but these tips should make it go more smoothly.

## TIP 123

## Don't Ask Employees, Friends, or Family Members for Reviews if You Haven't Treated Them

Like I have previously mentioned, you should only ask friends and family for reviews if you have treated them. Google and Yelp are tracking you and they know how to leave reviews.

If you want to appear as a credible business online, you must be a credible business.

Don't take shortcuts.

Treat your patients well and they will talk about you online. Their testimonials will go a lot further typically, too, as they're writing the review of their own volition as a happy customer of your business. They aren't being coaxed into it or doing it as a favor—they're writing about real scenarios they've deemed to be worth raving about.

# TIP 124

## Don't Panic and Stress Out Over One Bad Review

Negative reviews happen to every business.

Unfortunately, people who had a negative experience at a business are much more likely to go online and write a negative review than people who have had a positive experience.

This is why I always try to leave positive reviews for businesses when I get the opportunity.

Then again, I've written books on this stuff and I'm going to care a lot more than the average patient.

Most don't want to be inconvenienced by writing a review unless they're ticked off enough to need to vent or "get back" at you.

Panicking is the worst things you can do. Instead, follow the other tips on how to handle it.

Stressing out is equally as bad, as it does no good for you. And going through your day stressed could cause you or your team to make errors with other patients and earn other bad reviews!

## TIP 125

### Don't "Gate" Reviews

Years ago, you were allowed to "gate" your reviews by first asking for a review and then only asking people who submit positive reviews to share it on Google.

Practice owners would use software to "gate" reviews, sending a request for patients to indicate whether they had a positive or negative experience. Those who indicated they had a negative experience got redirected to submit feedback directly to the practice only. Those who indicated they had a positive experience got redirected to a form that allowed them to easily post a public online review.

Not only does review gating violate Google's terms, risking reviews disappearing and losing trust with patients and prospective patients, but it's also unnecessary. If you use the other tips in this book to ensure you collect a steady stream of positive reviews, an occasional negative review will be quickly pushed down by all the positive ones. And an occasional negative review will add more credibility to the positive ones.

To learn more about Google's gating policy and Birdeye's stance on gating visit https://birdeye.com/blog/google-birdeye-against-review-gating/.

# CONCLUSION

At the end of the day, if you want to grow your practice and build a well-known name for yourself and your practice, you need to start implementing these strategies to get more reviews.

It can be challenging when you don't know where to start, but now that you have read this book, you can begin with day one, tip one, and start implementing these strategies today.

Having a ton of good reviews and a good ranking on Google will improve your SEO and will help bring in more patients.

I have been helping dentists like you grow your practice since 2013 and have put the best (and simplest) proven strategies on how to get more reviews in this book.

My passion is to help you attain the dental practice of your dreams. I have not only been where you are now, but I have grown my practice to where I wanted it to go and have helped many other dentists do the same.

The strategies and tips in this book have been proven to work in getting more reviews and therefore more patients.

I didn't get the nickname the "Reputation Doctor" for nothing. Start today and watch as you gain more reviews and patients.

For even more help, visit DrLenTau.com, email me at Len@DrLenTau.com, or just pick up the phone and call me at (215) 292-2100. Yes, I'm putting my cell phone number in the book. Use it.

Between my books, consulting, and my podcast, I offer several ways to help.

You work hard enough.

It's time to make your life a little easier.

And, if you want to see my recommended resources to help you grow your practice, visit the page linked to this QR code.

# ACKNOWLEDGMENTS

When I wrote my first book, *Raving Patients: The Definitive Guide To Using Reputation Marketing To Attract Hundreds Of New Patients*, I did so with the goal of helping practice owners create a steady flow of new patients to their practice through reputation marketing.

In this book, my goal is to give practice owners a collection of tips they can implement right away to make collecting and promoting online reviews easy.

Like my last book, this book would not have been possible without the help of a lot of people who contributed their time, tips, and talents to helping make this book a reality.

Here they are, in no particular order: Dr. Glenn Vo, creator of NiftyThriftyDentists.com, for writing the Foreword along with all the Pro Tip contributors, Sonny Spera, Josh Bernstein, Jeremy Krell, Jason Lipscomb, Bryan Laskin, Adam Zilko, Doc Hoffpauir, Paul Goodman, Gina Dorfman, Scott Childress, Joanne Block Rief, Eric Moryoussef, Joshua Austin, Minal Sampat, Meenal Patel, Nathan Ho, Evan Lazarus, Allison Lacoursiere.

Thank you for making this book better. I appreciate you and your valuable contributions.

Thank you, again, to my wonderful wife, Risa. In *Raving Patients*, I thanked you in my first book for the patience, dedication, support, and love that allowed me to shift my career from full-time clinical dentistry to part-time clinical dentistry, speaking, consulting, podcasting, writing, and selling Birdeye. Since then, you've continued to support me, sacrifice for our family, put up with all of my loud calls and Zoom, and more. You've enabled us to move our family from Philadelphia to Florida and helped me confidently sell my practice to my associate to focus even more time on speaking, consulting, podcasting, writing, selling Birdeye, and making even more loud calls and Zoom meetings. You are my inspiration and the greatest supporter I could ask for. I love you more than words can express.

Thank you to my son, Aidan. Your mother and I are incredibly proud of the happy, funny, and bright man you have become. You take so much pride in everything you do, from schoolwork to tennis. And you are the best friend, son, and grandson anyone could ever ask for. You make parenting easy for your mother and me. You are everything I dreamed of when I thought about having a son, and more.

Thank you, again, to Nick Pavlidis and Authority Ghostwriting. I know people don't typically acknowledge the person who helped you get the book to the finish line, but, as with *Raving Patients*, Nick, and his team members Ethan Webb, Hailey DeFaria, Jeff Anderton, and Kate Matson helped me organize my tips and get this book over the finish line. Thanks, Nick, for your continued support and helping me get these tips into the hands of the practice owners who need it.

And, to my patients, consulting clients, and attendees of my seminars—thank you for trusting me to help you over the years.

# ABOUT THE AUTHOR

Chosen as one of the top leaders in dental consulting by *Dentistry Today*, Len Tau, DMD, has dedicated his professional life to improving dentistry for both patients and other dentists.

After purchasing his practice, the Pennsylvania Center for Dental Excellence in Philadelphia, in 2007, Len practiced full-time while consulting to other dental practices, training thousands of dentists about reputation marketing, leading the dental division of Birdeye, a reputation marketing platform, and hosting the popular "Raving Patients" podcast.

In 2018, Len cut down to practicing dentistry two days per week to focus additional time and attention on helping other dentists build online footprints that attract hundreds of new patients to their practices. He has since sold his practice to his associate so he can concentrate on clinical care and helping other practice owners. He continues to practice two days per week.

Len lectures nationally and internationally on using internet marketing, social media, and reputation marketing to make dental offices more visible and credible as well as how to increase their case acceptance. In 2020, Len published his first book, *Raving Patients: The Definitive Guide To Using Reputation Marketing To Attract Hundreds Of New Patients*, which shares simple tips and best practices to become visible and demonstrate credibility online.

In addition to being the General Manager of the Dental Division for Birdeye, Len is the founder of Tau Dental Consulting, a consulting firm that helps dentists develop a comprehensive online marketing plan.

His content-rich, engaging seminars allow him to bring his firsthand experiences to his audiences. He lives in Florida with his wife, Risa, and son, Aidan, and commutes to Philadelphia two days a week to serve patients.

To connect with Len, visit DrLenTau.com, email him at Len@DrLenTau.com, or just text or call him on his cell phone, (215) 292-2100.

Made in the USA
Columbia, SC
18 March 2025